Make & Give

Simple and Modern Crafts to Brighten Every Day

By STEPH HUNG & ERIN JANG

ROOST
BOOKS

Boston & London
2014

Library of Congress
Cataloging-in-Publication Data

Hung, Steph. Make and give: simple
and modern crafts to brighten
every day / Steph Hung and Erin Jang. —
First edition. pages   cm
ISBN 978-1-61180-148-4 (alk. paper)
1. Handicraft. 2. Gifts.
I. Jang, Erin. II. Title.
TT880.H854 2014
745.5—dc23
2014013452

Distributed in
the United States by
Penguin Random House
LLC and in Canada
by Random House of
Canada Ltd

9 8 7 6 5 4 3 2 1
First Edition
Printed in the United States of America

This edition is printed on acid-free paper
that meets the American National Standards
Institute Z39.48 Standard.

Shambhala Publications makes every
effort to print on recycled paper.
For more information please visit
www.shambhala.com.

Roost Books
An imprint of
Shambhala Publications, Inc.
Horticultural Hall
300 Massachusetts Avenue
Boston, Massachusetts 02115
roostbooks.com

Designed
by Erin Jang
Cover photograph
by Dan Wonderly
Photographs by
Erin Jang

Table of Contents

Introduction

A **TOKEN OF AFFECTION** means the most when it is handmade and heartfelt. It's **THE SMALL THINGS** that pack the most punch: a secret note, a sweet treat, or or a little gift to brighten the day. Nothing brings a smile to someone's face like the **ELEMENT OF SURPRISE**: an unexpected gesture that makes them feel special.

As an art director (Erin) and craft editor (Steph) at *Martha Stewart Living*, we quickly bonded over our mutual love of making gifts for **FRIENDS AND FAMILY**. Over photo shoot lunches, we'd share our own personal projects—a surprise farmers' market lunch packed for a friend, an embroidered pillow for a new baby, a handmade book illustrated for a nephew's first birthday. **A CONSIDERED GIFT**, one that is thoughtful to the recipient, always leaves a lasting impression. It doesn't have to be extravagant, expensive, or take all weekend to make — what counts is taking the time to remember those little details about them and WHAT THEY LOVE (like their favorite color, candy, flower, or sports team).

The crafts here were designed for any occasion and EVERYDAY USE, because you don't need a birthday or holiday to show how much you care. With the help of some clever new materials and MODERN TWISTS on commonly used items, we created these projects with the intention of minimum effort for maximum effect.

We hope our book will inspire you to MAKE AND GIVE something, and make someone smile.

To the Reader

Designed for our nearest and dearest, the crafts in this book all have fond personal memories attached to them. We hope you use this book as a guide for your own occasions. Each project has a "Make this for" section to use as a launching point to inspire you to make something for the people you love.

HERE ARE SOME OF OUR PERSONAL EXAMPLES

Erin:

	HUSBAND	SON	IN-LAWS
WHO?	HUSBAND	SON	IN-LAWS
WHY?	long week at work	first day of preschool	visiting
WHAT DO THEY LIKE?	coffee, biking, reading the news	toys, snacks, drawing, animals	fruit, playing mah-jongg, spending time with grandchildren
LESS TIME?	Coffee Sampler	Fill-in-the-Blank Tattoos, Everyday Advent	Farmers' Market Gifts, Thank-You Wallet
MORE TIME?	Voracious Reader Tote, Bike Dates	Secret Love Note Shirt, Tangram Prints, Trompe L'oeil Shoes	Candy Board Games, Hand-Drawn Pillows (with a drawing of them by their grandson)

1
Who is the
gift for?

2
Why do you
want to make
them a gift?

3
What do
they like?

4
How much
time do
you have?

Steph:			
WHO?	**BEST BUD**	**COUSIN**	**MOM**
WHY?	potluck dinner	going to college	Sunday afternoon
WHAT DO THEY LIKE?	beer, games, looking sharp at work	bright colors, decorating her room	high tea, feeling fancy
LESS TIME?	Scratch-Off Calendar	Day & Night Clock Face	Flower Pun Bouquets
MORE TIME?	Custom Growler, Nickname Handkerchiefs, Fortune Tree	Accordion Cards, Unofficial Business Cards, Rebus Wall Hanging	Macaron Messages, Lavender Cloud Sachets, Tea Sampler

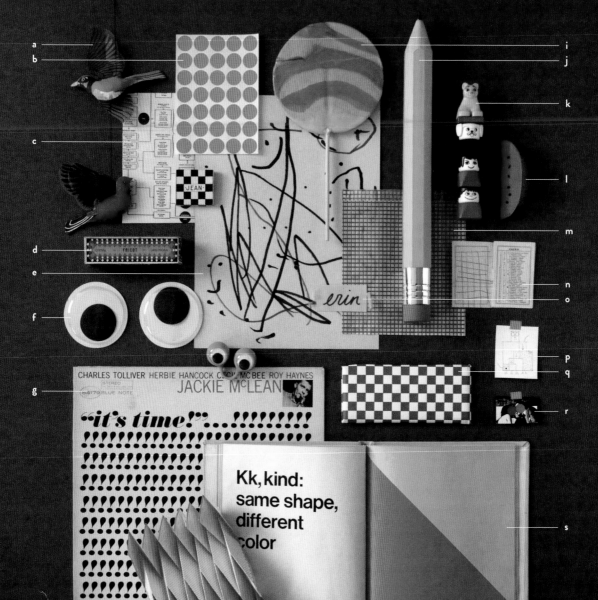

a

b

c

d

e

f

g

CHARLES TOLLIVER   HERBIE HANCOCK   CECIL McBEE   ROY HAYNES
JACKIE McLEAN
STEREO
(84179 BLUE NOTE

"it's time!"...!!!!!

h

i

j

k

l

m

n

o

p

q

r

Kk, kind:
same shape,
different
color

s

erin

Erin's Inspiration

Here are some things that inspire us and led to the projects within this book.

(1) I love the clever design and graphic shapes found on JAZZ ALBUM COVERS (g), CHILDREN'S BOOKS (like this one by Donald Crews) (s), and CANDY BAR WRAPPERS (q) by Chocolate Editions.

(2) Information is much more fun when it's packaged as an INFOGRAPHIC (c). Our book is designed with lots of useful charts, formulas, and tips to help you begin a project.

(3) I love PACKAGING SUPPLIES (m), and often a project is born when I discover a cool-shaped box, a fun party container, or a great bag. We developed our *Housewarming Gift* project after finding white gable boxes that look just like houses!

(4) Often I think a drawing my son Miles has done (e) would make a great textile print. We turned some HOMEMADE ART into our *Hand-Drawn Pillows* project.

(5) ANTIQUE STORES AND FLEA MARKETS are some of my favorite places to find inspiration (d). My beloved vintage bird mobile (a) led to our *Rebus Wall Hanging*. PAPER EPHEMERA is another favorite of mine, and this tiny pocket calendar I found in Spain (n) came to mind when we designed our *Scratch-Off Calendar*.

(6) I love my husband's messy HANDWRITING, and I save every note he gives me (o). There's something special about the way someone writes your name. We embrace that quality in our *Nickname Handkerchiefs*.

(7) SAUL STEINBERG'S ARTWORK always makes me smile. This whimsical family picture (p) came to mind as we thought of a clever way to represent the family portrait in our *Family Tree Embroidery* project.

(8) GOOGLY EYES (f) make everyone happy. Steph jokes that I would add them to every project if I could. We found a place to include them in one of our *Ultimate Desk Surprise* projects!

(9) I can spend hours in an old OFFICE SUPPLY STORE looking for a particular neon label or type of sticker paper. These round labels (b) remind me of one of my favorite artists, JOHN BALDESSARI (r); both inspired our *Neon Photo Postcards*.

(10) I always think of a new craft idea whenever I visit ECONOMY CANDY, my favorite candy shop in New York, and leave with a cool treat like this giant lollipop (i). We came up with a couple projects after a visit there (*Candy Board Games* and *Cake Portraits*).

(11) CHILDREN'S TOYS can be so graphic and fun. I love the playful scale of this giant pencil (j), the funny faces on Miles's vintage Duplo blocks (k), and the shapes of his fake play food (l).

(12) In my design work, I like using UNUSUAL PAPER FOLDS AND DIMENSIONS (h). Our *Accordion Cards*, *Perpetual Greeting*, and *Thank-You Wallet* play with scale, shape, and interesting folds.

a

b

c

d

e

f

g

h

i

j

k

l

m

n

o

p

q

r

s

Steph's Inspiration

1 I love the vintage quality and bright lines of these AIRMAIL ENVELOPES (q) I found in a stationery shop in Chinatown. We tried to mimic their simple, yet bold border in our *Neon Photo Postcards*.

2 The nap pillows I made for a craft fair with these LIBERTY OF LONDON FABRICS (i) led to the *Hand-Drawn Pillows*, which are also the right size for cuddling on a couch.

3 Felt is one of my favorite fabrics because it is tactile, easy to handle, and doesn't fray. *Lavender Cloud Sachets* always remind me of this POCKET-SIZED ELEPHANT (l), a prized gift from a best friend.

4 Coral & Tusk (one of my favorite companies and run by a genius crafter) makes the most incredible SEWN DRAWINGS (m) and inspired our own stitched art in *Family Tree Embroidery*.

5 I recently visited PARIS for the first time and found the city completely magical (k). Its beautiful streets were full of romance and the patisseries were stocked with treats—memories we tried to evoke in *Macaron Messages*.

6 FORTUNE FISH (g) are so much fun, as is the thrill of reading horoscopes. (I'm a Capricorn!) We wanted to evoke that same excited feeling with our *Fortune Tree*.

7 Office desks and work spaces can often be dull so we like to brighten the mood with fun supplies like these ANIMAL PAPER CLIPS (n), which led to our idea for assembling *The Ultimate Desk Surprise*.

8 Nature is one of my greatest inspirations, and a walk outdoors often ends with a new treasure—whether it is a BIRD'S FEATHER (h), a simple STONE (a), a CRYSTAL (f), or a few tiny SEASHELLS (e). Every landscape has its own distinct elements and every season its bounty, something we tried to capture in our *Farmers' Market Gifts*.

9 My most prized possessions are handmade gifts like these BEADED (r) AND KNIT NECKLACES (c), and I think of my dear friends each time I wear one. Stylish gifts like our *Trompe L'oeil Shoes* and *Voracious Reader Tote* will also remind someone that they are loved whenever they wear them.

10 Simple embellishments like these RIBBON FLAGS (b) (mementos from my first photo shoot at *Martha Stewart Living*) show that even the smallest touch will put the extra in the ordinary, just like our *Flower Pun Bouquets*.

11 As a kid I used to spend weekend mornings with my brother watching cartoons, and playing CARDS (s) and games. We would have been so excited to challenge each other over *Candy Board Games*.

12 I love anything with small compartments, like this old LABORATORY PALETTE (o) and the pillbox used in our *Everyday Advent*.

Materials

We like working with everyday items — things you can easily find in an office store, a party supply shop, a supermarket, or your home. We've organized all our materials here by category, for your reference. As visual people, it helps us to see everything we need before we begin a craft. That's why we've also designed an "ingredient" list of necessary materials on the first page of each project. Turn to the next section for our favorite supplies and their sources.

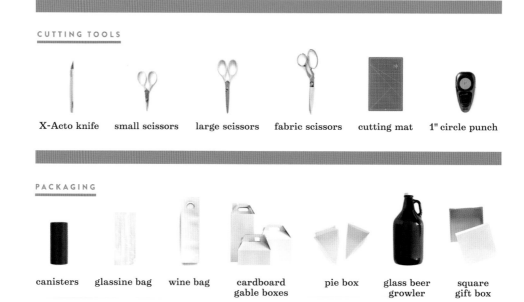

CUTTING TOOLS

X-Acto knife   small scissors   large scissors   fabric scissors   cutting mat   1" circle punch

PACKAGING

canisters   glassine bag   wine bag   cardboard gable boxes   pie box   glass beer growler   square gift box

FOOD

macarons

coffee beans

tea bags

herbs

candy

traditional
housewarming
gifts

plain round
iced cake

farmers'
market fruit

snacks

food-safe
markers

muffin

FLORAL

lavender

flowers

wire cutters

floral wire

houseplant

floral wire stems

FASHION

canvas shoes

T-shirt

handkerchiefs

tote bag

FABRIC & SEWING

sewing machine | cotton webbing | fabric | felt | water soluble marker | embroidery hoops | iron

embroidery floss | velcro strips | thread | sewing needle | sewing pins | pillow stuffing

OFFICE

ink pad | binder clips | label maker | screw punch | dry-erase markers | marker | notebook

office labels | letter decals | letter stencils | chalk | ruler | bone folder | pen

split pins | stamp set | vinyl pouch | sticky notes

envelopes

blank board book

cardstock

label paper

printer paper

colored paper

tattoo paper

adhesive dry-erase sheets

cardboard

iron-on transfer paper

transparency paper

printed photos

foam core board

bristol board

newspaper

blank business cards

honeycomb paper

CD paper sleeves

heavy books and cardboard sheets

crinkle shredded paper

crepe paper

Con-Tact paper

parchment paper

17

petri
dishes

water
balloons

balloon
pump

scratch-off
labels

googly eyes

wooden
dowel

gift
cards

square
lacquer tray

picture
frame

rubber
printing block

vintage photos
and postcards

awl

clock

small toys

paper towel

large pillbox

drawings

rattail
cord

vending
capsules

tea towels

PAINT

gouache paint   foam brush   paint pouncer   multisurface
craft paint

TAPE & ADHESIVE

painters' tape   glow-in-the-
dark tape   spray
adhesive   tape   double-stick
tape   white glue

adhesive
dots   glue stick

Our Favorite Supplies

SMALL MARTHA STEWART CRAFTS SCISSORS
These handy snippers can tackle any tight corner with their sharp points. *shop .marthastewart.com*

FOOD-SAFE MARKERS
The edible ink in these markers makes it possible to share a special message on a sweet treat. *www.whisknyc.com*

GLOW-IN-THE-DARK TAPE
Found in most photography supply shops, this tape is easier than using paint because of its adhesive backing. *www.setshop.com*

WATER-SOLUBLE MARKER
This ingenious tool is a boon for precision cutting and sewing. *www.amazon.com*

GLUE DOTS
A cross between glue and tape, these dots are easy to apply and mess-free. *www .paperpresentation.com*

HONEYCOMB PAPER
Complex folds and layers make even the simplest dimensional shapes look interesting. *www .devra-party.com*

VENDING CAPSULES
We love these colorful containers because they are inexpensive and perfect for holding any kind of small treat, toy, or message. *www.heyyoyo.com*

SCREW PUNCH
This indispensable tool can make holes in various sizes anywhere on a page. *shop.marthastewart.com*

EMBROIDERY FLOSS
We like how its strands can be separated so we can control the thickness of our stitches when sewing. *www.herrschners.com*

OFFICE SUPPLIES
We are always on the lookout for unusual or vintage versions of paper, envelopes, pens, and labels on our scouting trips and travels.

TATTOO PAPER
We still can't believe how simple it is to make our own tattoos with a basic home computer and inkjet printer. *www.decalpaper.com*

ALPHABET STENCILS
The paper versions are affordable and come in an array of sizes, in classic letterforms that are graphic designer–approved. *www .homedepot.com*

SCRATCH-OFF LABELS
Every day is lottery day with these innovative stickers, which come in gold, silver, and even holographic versions! *www .myscratchofflabels.com*

CANDY
Candy is a guaranteed way to make anyone happy. We love that it is simple, inexpensive, and comes in every size, shape, and color imaginable.

PACKAGING
Many of our projects have been inspired by packaging basics such as bags, gift boxes, and even takeout containers.

STAMP SET
We like to add an extra touch by personalizing our gifts. We love the simple and clean look of the letters in these rubber office stamps. *www .staples.com*

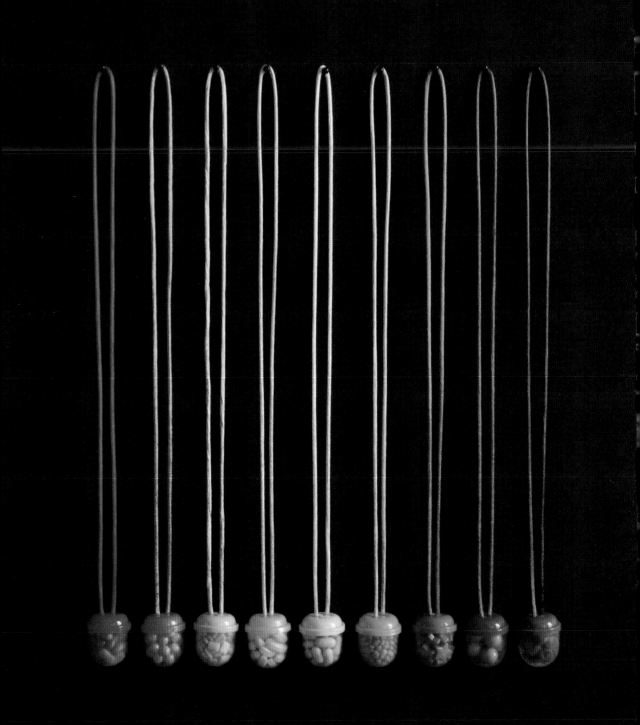

Candy Capsule Necklaces

Like most kids, Erin's nephews flip over candy jewelry and especially love to show off those sweet, edible gems. We put a little twist on their beloved treats by filling these vending capsules with their favorite candies and stringing them onto brightly colored cords. Unlike sticky lollipop rings, our necklaces keep little hands clean, the candy can be saved for later, and the capsules can always be refilled.

Materials:

1" plastic vending capsules + awl + 1 yard of 2-mm rattail cord *(we like to match the cord color to the capsule lid)* + scissors + tape + small candy

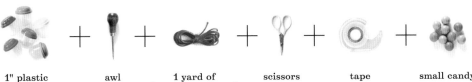

MAKE THIS FOR → classroom party treat | best friend's sweet tooth | niece's charm necklace

Steps:

1. Use the awl to punch two holes (¼" apart) in the capsule lid.

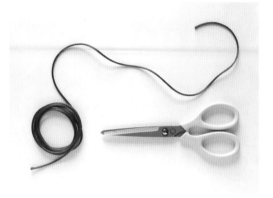

2. Cut the cord to 30" length.

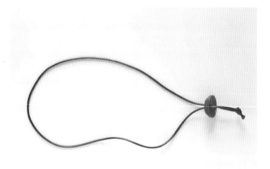

3. Thread the cord ends through the holes in the capsule lid. (You may find it helpful to wrap the cord ends with tape to make stiffer tips.) Make a knot on the inside of the lid. Trim ends with scissors.

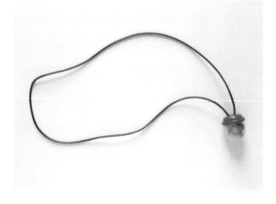

4. Fill the capsule with candy and snap on the lid.

Sweets Glossary

Fill these rings with a variety of small candies—here are just a few of our favorite treats!

**SOUR CHERRY
GUMMIES**

**CINNAMON
HEARTS**

**CANDY-COATED
SUNFLOWER SEEDS**

**PINK AND ORANGE
SIXLETS**

**SOUR LEMON
NERDS**

BANANA RUNTS

**MINI GUMMY
BEARS**

**TINY
CHICLETS GUM**

**GREEN
SIXLETS**

**LIME
JELLY BEANS**

**GREEN
CANDY STARS**

JUJUBES

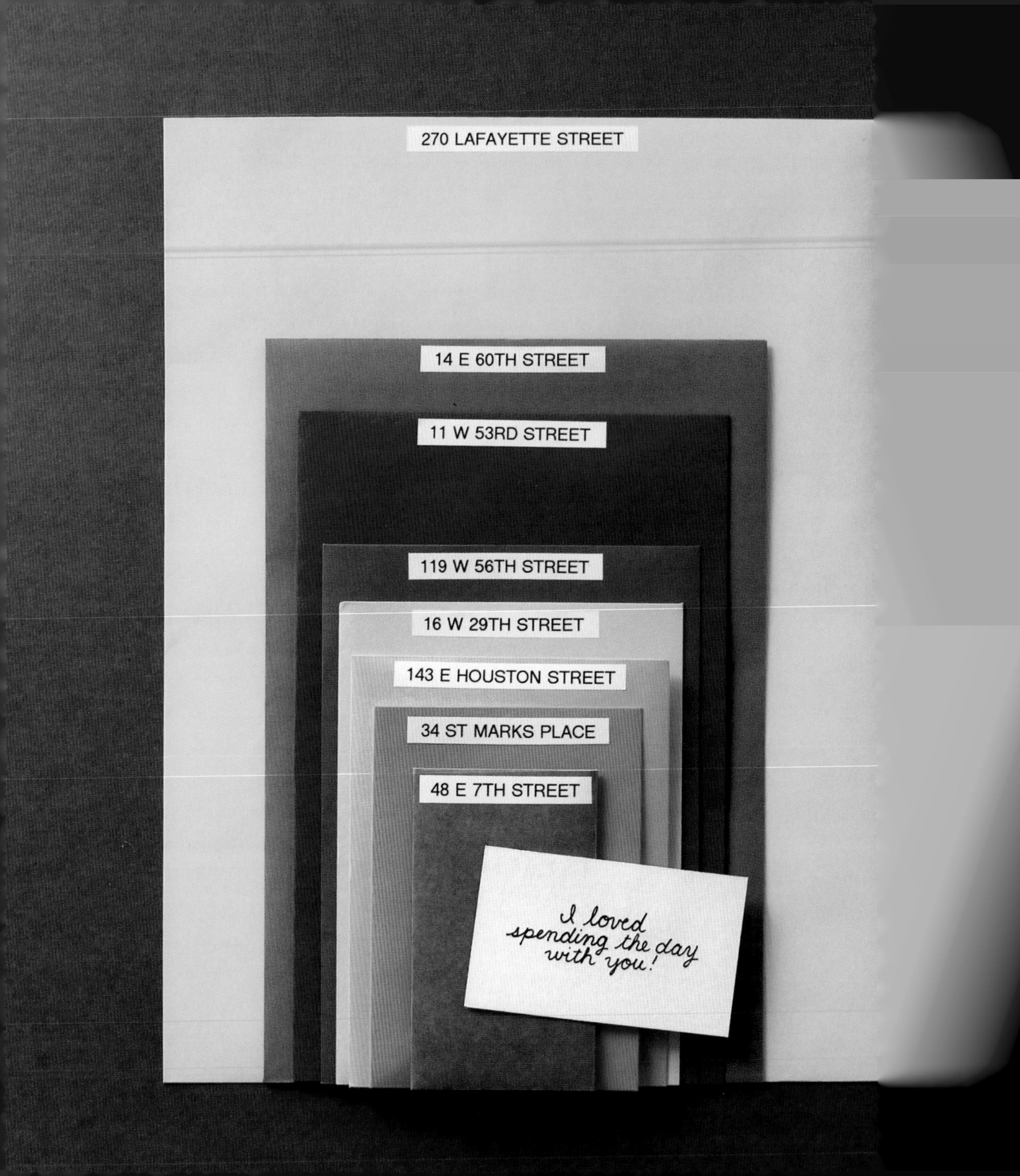

270 LAFAYETTE STREET

14 E 60TH STREET

11 W 53RD STREET

119 W 56TH STREET

16 W 29TH STREET

143 E HOUSTON STREET

34 ST MARKS PLACE

48 E 7TH STREET

I loved
spending the day
with you!

Progressive Date

We always prefer a fun experience over a fancy gift. For her husband's birthday, Erin told him to keep an entire Saturday free, then planned an itinerary around the places she knew he would love (a great coffee shop, a hole-in-the-wall eatery, a new exhibit at the art museum, a movie he'd wanted to see). Much like a scavenger hunt, he was only given the first address and received the next one at each destination. The presentation of hidden, nested envelopes added another layer of surprise at each stop of the day.

Materials:

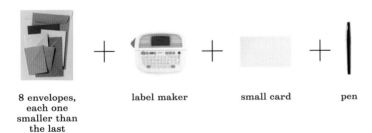

8 envelopes, each one smaller than the last   +   label maker   +   small card   +   pen

MAKE THIS FOR → wedding anniversary | best friend in town for one day | Mother's Day

Steps:

1. Print labels for eight different locations. These will be the stopping points for the date. Adhere to envelopes in the order of your route (first destination on the largest envelope, and so on).
2. Write a personal note on the card, which will be revealed at the last destination.
3. Seal the card in the smallest envelope, place it in the next sized envelope, and so on.

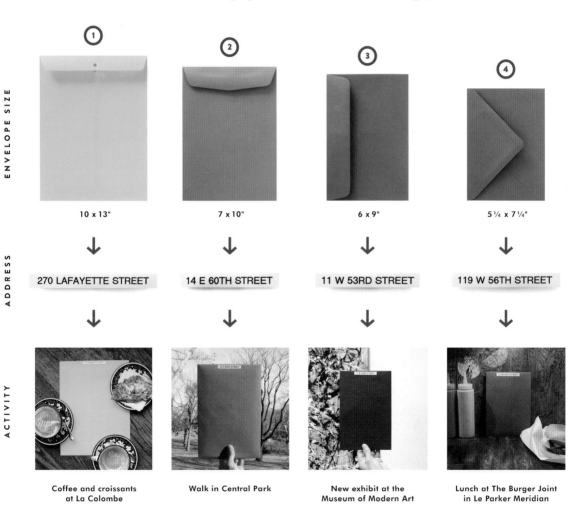

ENVELOPE SIZE

1	2	3	4
10 x 13"	7 x 10"	6 x 9"	5 ¼ x 7 ¼"

ADDRESS

270 LAFAYETTE STREET · 14 E 60TH STREET · 11 W 53RD STREET · 119 W 56TH STREET

ACTIVITY

Coffee and croissants at La Colombe · Walk in Central Park · New exhibit at the Museum of Modern Art · Lunch at The Burger Joint in Le Parker Meridian

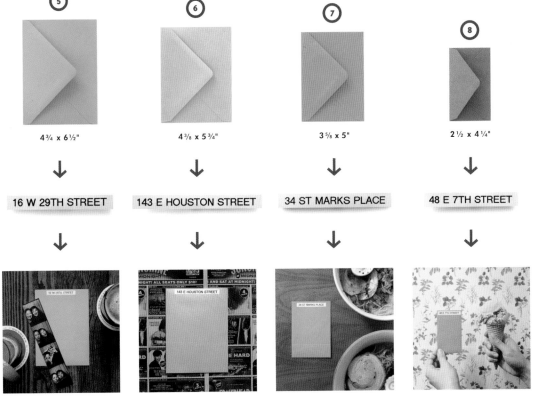

5

4³⁄₄ x 6¹⁄₂"

↓

16 W 29TH STREET

↓

Photobooth fun at
the Ace Hotel, followed by
cocktails at The Breslin

6

4³⁄₈ x 5³⁄₄"

↓

143 E HOUSTON STREET

↓

A movie at
Sunshine Cinema

7

3⁵⁄₈ x 5"

↓

34 ST MARKS PLACE

↓

Dinner at Ramen Setagaya

8

2¹⁄₂ x 4¹⁄₄"

↓

48 E 7TH STREET

↓

A scoop of ice cream
at Van Leeuwen

You're my sweetpea.

Turn to page 33 to see our suggestions for stem/sentiment pairings!

Flower Pun Bouquets

Say it with flowers! A gift of fresh blooms is a classic way to show someone you care. Steph likes to keep things simple by giving single variety bouquets because they make a strong statement. Plus, they're always available at the corner bodega for a last-minute pickup! We add a little wordplay with our speech balloon templates, so these colorful stems are sure to make anyone smile.

Materials:

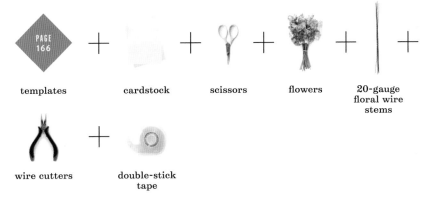

templates + cardstock + scissors + flowers + 20-gauge floral wire stems +

wire cutters + double-stick tape

MAKE THIS FOR → airport pickup | makeup after a breakup | secret admirer

Steps:

1. Print the templates onto cardstock. Cut out the front and back of the speech bubble to make a double-sided sign. (For a perfect match, cut the tips first, line them up, and cut the speech bubbles together.)

2. Trim the floral wire to the length of the flowers.

3. Lay one end of the floral wire on the back of a speech bubble and secure it with double-stick tape. Adhere both sides of the speech bubble together.

4. Tuck it inside either a store-bought flower bouquet, a potted plant, or a vase arrangement.

LOOK WHO'S TALKING!

Find a flower that speaks your mind.

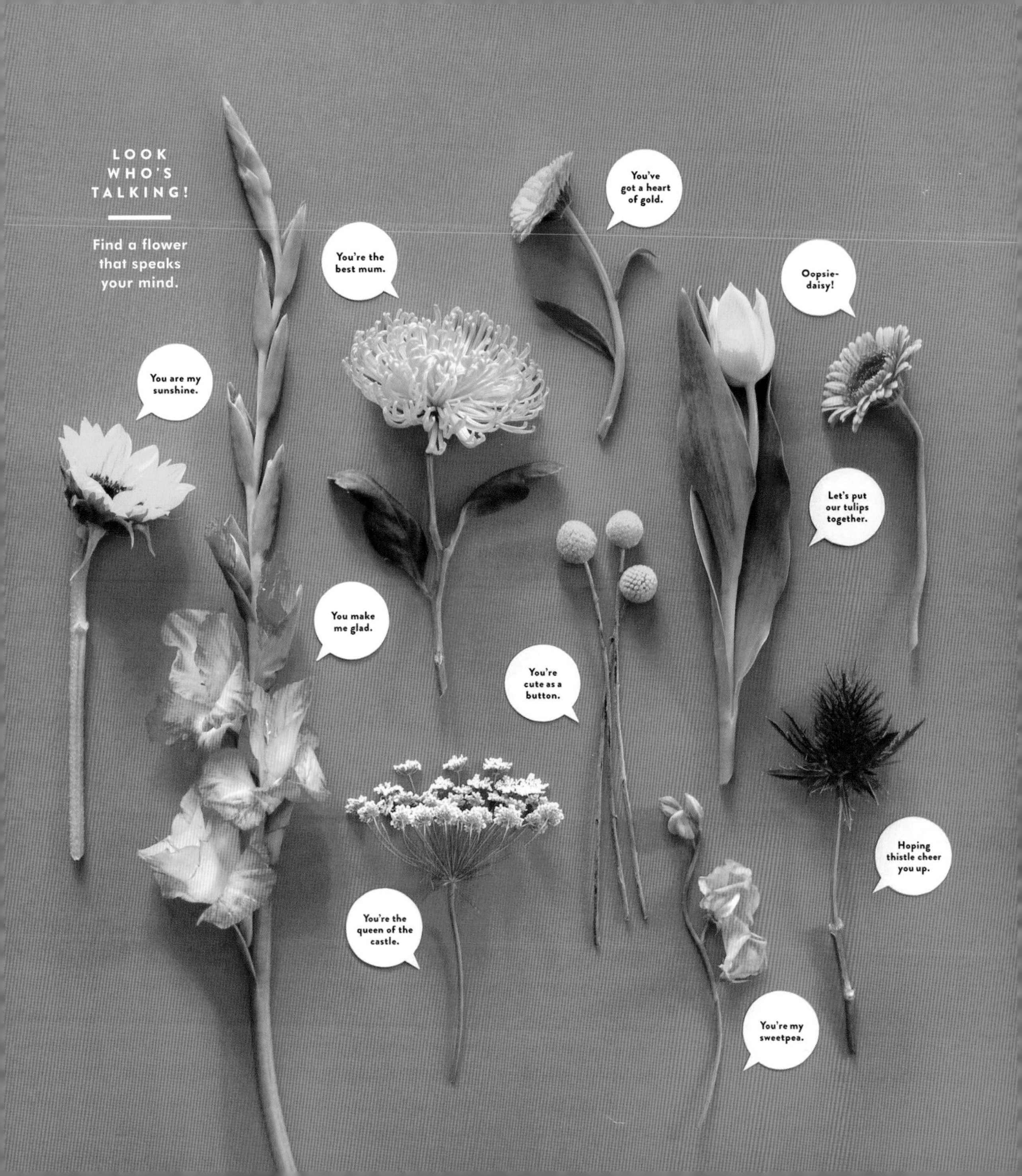

Fortune Tree

The best part of getting Chinese takeout with friends is opening up our fortune cookies. Bright balloons and playful fortunes make this tree full of lucky fruit. We took a simple houseplant (any sturdy one will do but we like to use a money tree) and fitted it with its own party trick. Surprise your friends with messages hidden inside the "oranges."

Materials:

printer paper + scissors + pen + orange water balloons + balloon pump + houseplant +

green paper + X-Acto knife + floral wire + wire cutters

MAKE THIS FOR → New Year's Eve | hostess gift | office party

Steps:

1. Cut thin strips of printer paper and write the fortunes. Insert a rolled fortune into the tip of a balloon.

2. Inflate the balloon with the pump and close it with a tight knot.

3. Trace one of the leaves from the tree onto green paper and cut leaves out. Make an X in the leaf tip using an X-Acto knife. Push the balloon tip through the X in the leaf.

4. Cut a 2" length of floral wire. Shape one end into a hook and tie the other end around the balloon tip. Hook the balloons onto the tree.

True love is on its way, so make room!

↑

**HOW DO
I LOVE THEE?**

Let me count the ways.
Instead of fortunes,
write down all the reasons
why you love someone
and tuck each message
into a balloon.

Fill-in-the-Blank Tattoos

Our nephews and nieces love temporary tattoos and would easily fill their arms with them if allowed. As a special gift for them, we like to make our own. We created these fill-in-the-blank designs that can be customized to suit any mood, interest, and imagination. They make a playful present for the creative child, wannabe tattoo artist, or anyone who likes to doodle.

Materials:

PAGE 167	+		+		+		+	
templates		tattoo paper		scissors		paper towel		marker*

MAKE THIS FOR → | tailgate party | neighborhood BBQ | end-of-year classroom party

*We use nontoxic permanent markers for the best results, since the ink never comes in contact with skin. But feel free to use washable markers if you prefer.

Steps:

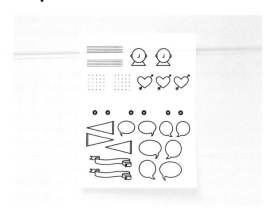

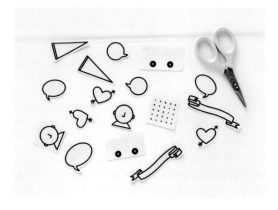

1. Print the templates onto tattoo paper and apply the cover paper according to the manufacturer's instructions.

2. Cut out the tattoos along the dotted lines if provided, or closely around each design.

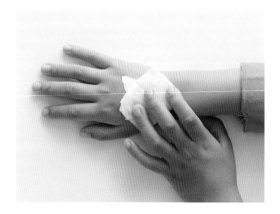

3. Peel off the cover paper and place the tattoo facedown on the skin. Moisten a paper towel with water and wet the tattoo completely, being careful not to move it.

4. Once the tattoo has adhered to the skin, the backing paper will slide off easily. Allow it to dry completely before filling in the designs with a marker.

Variety Show

There are countless ways to embellish our tattoos. Here are just a few ideas!

Write the name of your best friend, special someone, or your newest obsession.

Draw a superhero, the guest of honor at a party, or a super silly face!

Add a measure from a beloved tune, rock song, or sound track.

Add a personal motto or favorite expression.

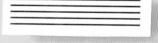

This word search is a fun activity for one, a few, or a party!

Draw a car, bike, construction digger, or a child's favorite subway train.

Fill in your signature exclamation: one word that best represents you.

Write your hometown, alma mater, or team pick for the Super Bowl!

I think
you're
dino-mite!

SUNDAY	MONDAY		WEDNESDAY	THURSDAY	FRIDAY	SATURDAY
S	M		W	T	F	S

Everyday Advent

When we were young, we could hardly wait until December 1 so we could pry open the first door of our advent calendars. We wanted to create something for our favorite children that would evoke the same feeling of excitement any day of the year. We also adore anything miniature, so looking for pint-sized treats to fit in these boxes was right up our alley.

Materials:

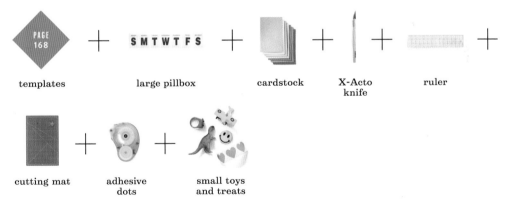

templates + large pillbox + cardstock + X-Acto knife + ruler +

cutting mat + adhesive dots + small toys and treats

MAKE THIS FOR → back-to-school blues | staycation | niece visiting from out of town

Steps:

1. Scale the templates to pillbox-lid size. Print and cut the cardstock with X-Acto knife, ruler, and cutting mat. (Alternatively, cut the cardstock to lid size and write your own small note on each paper.)

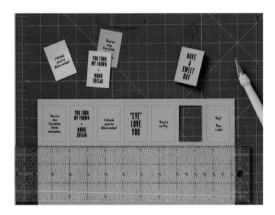

2. Attach each paper to a lid with an adhesive dot.

3. Place small toys and treats into each compartment.

Offer someone a daily coupon
that is worth a special treat or break.
(See page 168 for templates.)

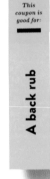
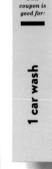

1 hour of quiet time

A back rub

1 car wash

Breakfast in bed

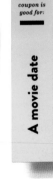

A coffee break

A movie date

2 loads of laundry

2

Pair a funny phrase with a silly toy to make someone smile.
(See page 168 for templates.)

You're my favorite little monster.

YOU TURN MY FROWN ↓ UPSIDE DOWN

I think you're dino-mite!

"EYE" LOVE YOU

You're so fly.

HAVE A SWEET DAY

Yay! You rule!

 + + + + + +

| our favorite monster finger puppet | novelty buttons | dinosaur figurine | googly eye ring | toy airplane | colorful gumballs | stickers and temporary tattoos |

45

3

Give a different type of candy each day, all in someone's favorite color.

My dear child,

In mama's heart always.

Love follows you, little one,

Everywhere you go, my

Sweet, smiling Miles.

inside outside

Secret
Love Note Shirt

We are always looking for ways to let someone know we care, especially when we are apart. A small message that is personal, yet discreet, can mean so much. When her son started preschool, Erin wanted to give him a little note to keep close to his heart as reassurance that his mama was never far away. If you're stumped for what to write, try a simple acrostic poem using the person's name.

Materials:

T-shirt   iron-on   scissors   iron
                 transfer
                 paper

| MAKE THIS FOR | → | first day of preschool | sleepaway camp | long-distance boyfriend |

Steps:

1. Measure the space where the transfer will go. (We like placing it directly above the heart, where a chest pocket would be on a shirt.) Create a design that will fit within the desired parameters.

2. Print the design onto iron-on transfer paper and cut it out. **IMPORTANT**: Remember to reverse your design before printing! You can use a computer design program to flip your design horizontally.

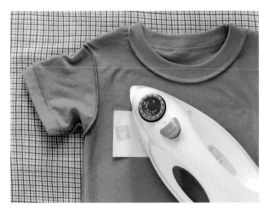

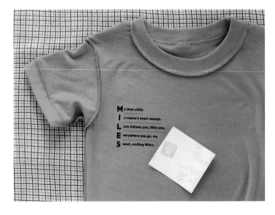

4. Heat-set the design with an iron according to manufacturer's instructions.

5. Peel off backing paper.

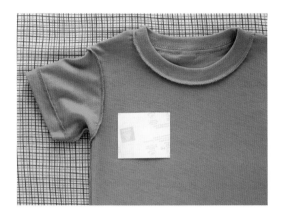

3. Turn the shirt inside out and lay it flat onto an ironing board. Position the design facedown onto the front of the T-shirt.

Tips:

Choose a shirt in a color that is both dark enough so you don't see the black text showing through, and light enough so you can still read the iron-on note.

Apply even pressure with the iron and make sure there is no water in the iron before you begin— steam is not your friend here!

Other application ideas include the underside of a necktie, inside a pocket lining, or the edge of a handkerchief.

cool

All About

JACOB!

(your name)

Personal Storybook

What child wouldn't love a personalized book? Not just a book with his or her name on the cover, but a whole book devoted to the things he or she likes to see, eat, and do. Erin has a tradition of making, writing, and illustrating a board book for her nieces and nephews on their first birthday. With that in mind, we developed this book with pages that can be rewritten as many times as children change their minds. A quick wipe of a cloth is all it takes to start with a clean page every time.

Materials:

PAGE 169	+	adhesive dry-erase sheets	+	scissors	+	6" × 6" board book	+	dry-erase markers

templates   adhesive dry-erase sheets   scissors   6" × 6" board book   dry-erase markers

MAKE THIS FOR →	long road trip	lazy Sunday indoors	afternoon with the grandparents

Steps:

1. Print templates onto adhesive dry-erase sheets.

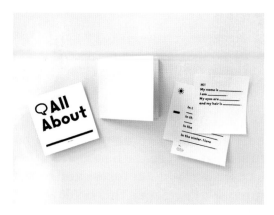

2. Cut out templates to page size.

3. Adhere templates to the board book.

4. Fill in the blanks using dry-erase markers. (See how Erin's nephew filled out his book on the next page!)

 **All About**
NATHAN

Hi!
My name is Nathan.
I am 5.
My eyes are brown
and my hair is crazy.

In the summer, I like swimming.
In the spring, I enjoy flying a kite.
In the fall, I go apple picking.
In the winter, I love the snow.

My family is mommy, daddy, Jacob and me.
We like to eat pizza together.
My friends are Jon, Ella, Marcy and Pete.
We like to play games together.

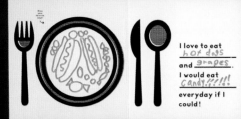
I love to eat hot dogs and grapes.
I would eat candy!!!!! everyday if I could!

I live in New York.
In my neighborhood I see trains and tall buildings.

When I grow up, I want to be an astronaut.
My dream is to go to space.

By ME !!!

to:
Dylan
from:
Erin
bright
COFFEE: Ethiopian Yirgacheffe
to:
Gina
from:
mellow
COFFEE:
to:
Julia
from:
Steph
sweet
COFFEE: Kenya AA
to:
Chris
from:
Erin
bold
COFFEE: French Roast
to:
Alex
from:
Steph
nutty
COFFEE: Sumatra
to:
Emily
from:
Steph
complex
COFFEE: Costa Rica

Coffee Sampler

This gift was created for the coffee purist: someone who travels with their own grinder, weighs their beans on a scale, and scoffs at flavored coffee. We like to match a coffee's distinguishing trait to our sweetheart's personality, to be given as a full-bodied compliment. Or give a pair of different blends to a coffee-drinking couple according to their contrasting and complementary personalities (for example, bold & mellow, nutty & sweet).

Materials:

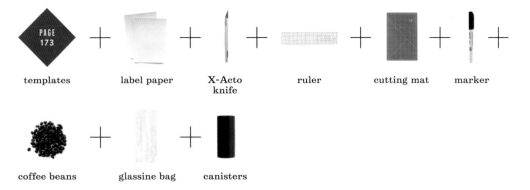

templates + label paper + X-Acto knife + ruler + cutting mat + marker +

coffee beans + glassine bag + canisters

MAKE THIS FOR → weekend brunch host | cram-session study buddy | coffee connoisseur couple

Steps:

1. Print templates onto label paper.

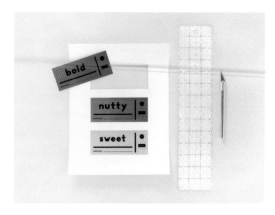

2. Cut out labels with an X-Acto knife, ruler, and cutting mat.

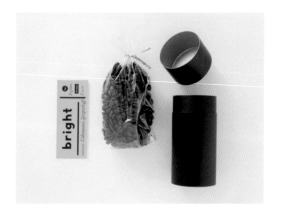

4. Package the coffee beans in glassine bags.

5. Place coffee beans in the canister and seal it with a label.

3. Write names and coffee types onto labels with a marker.

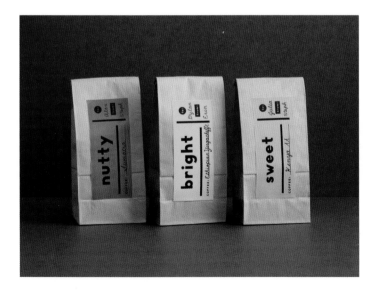

Tip:

While we love the look of black canisters, these labels will also look great with standard paper coffee bags.

Tea Sampler

When gifting tea we try to pair each blend with a specific mood, calling to mind the "Seven Dwarfs." Is a friend feeling sneezy? Give her ginger tea. Is a coworker feeling grumpy? Chamomile tea can ease his frown. Round acrylic containers and our funny face templates make for easy packaging. We like to give a set of seven teas for any mood or ailment.

Materials:

PAGE 174

templates + colored paper + scissors + petri dishes + adhesive dots + tea bags

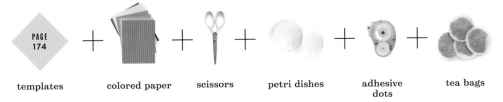

MAKE THIS FOR → sister's birthday | under-the-weather neighbor | care package

Steps:

1. Print templates onto paper.

2. Cut out front and back covers.

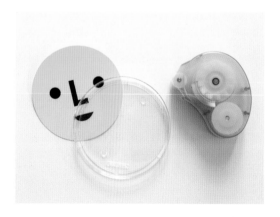

3. Attach front cover to the petri lid with an adhesive dot.

4. Lay back cover facedown onto the petri dish and fill it with tea bags. Close it with lid.

happy

Brighten up your mood with cheerful **LEMON TEA**.

LEMON TEA

dopey

Boost your sluggish memory and brain health with energizing **GREEN TEA**.

GREEN TEA

sleepy

Perk up with a perfect cup of **ENGLISH BREAKFAST TEA**.

ENGLISH BREAKFAST TEA

bashful

Tame your timid nerves with calming **LAVENDER TEA**.

LAVENDER TEA

doc

Remedy tummy troubles with **PEPPERMINT TEA** — it's just what the doctor ordered.

PEPPERMINT TEA

sneezy

Gesundheit!
Get rid of sniffles and sneezes with restorative **GINGER TEA**.

GINGER TEA

grumpy

Turn that frown upside down with soothing **CHAMOMILE TEA**.

CHAMOMILE TEA

A Tea for Every Occasion!

Taking a cue from the Seven Dwarfs, here are some common ailments and our suggested remedies. Store-bought tea bags will work, but you can also package loose bulk tea in small muslin bags.

Tangram Prints

A handmade stamp instantly transforms blank paper and fabric into a unique gift. With a single rubber block, you can create a menagerie of animals. The framed print shown was made for Steph's little cousin, who adores bunnies. Quite fittingly, he was also born in the Year of the Rabbit!

Materials:

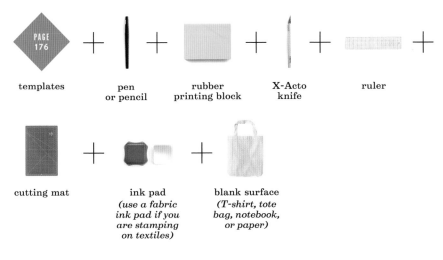

templates + pen or pencil + rubber printing block + X-Acto knife + ruler

cutting mat + ink pad (*use a fabric ink pad if you are stamping on textiles*) + blank surface (*T-shirt, tote bag, notebook, or paper*)

MAKE THIS FOR → custom greeting cards | baby's onesie | pair of pillowcases

Steps:

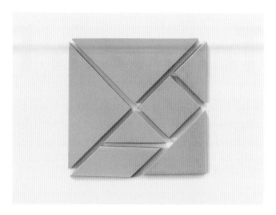

1. Draw lines on your rubber block according to our tangram template.

2. Use an X-Acto knife to cut out tangram blocks. To ensure the cleanest edges apply even pressure and make one solid stroke per line.

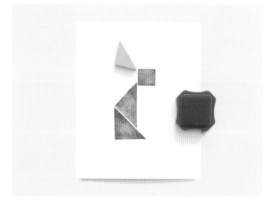

3. Press individual tangram blocks into the ink pad. Or you can also try pressing the ink pad onto each block for more control of the ink distribution.

4. Following the diagrams provided, stamp your animal designs onto a surface. Place something bigger on top of the block (like a stiff book) and press to ensure even pressure and a clean imprint.

Animal Kingdom

Use these as a guide for your stamped creations, or invent your own abstract designs!

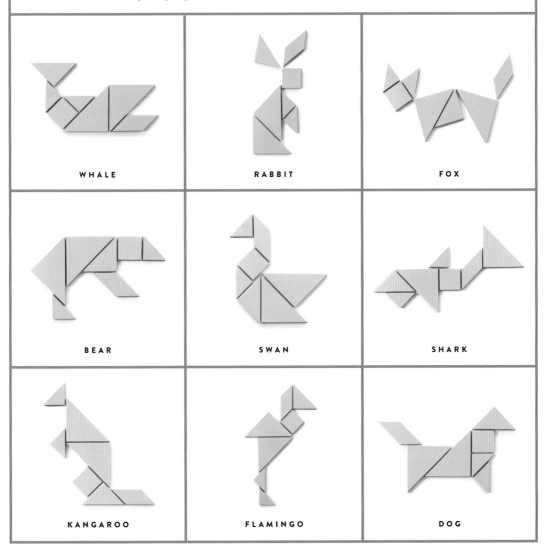

WHALE

RABBIT

FOX

BEAR

SWAN

SHARK

KANGAROO

FLAMINGO

DOG

Candy Board Games

A bowl of candy on the coffee table is always a welcome sight for a sweet tooth. We wanted to combine this with the whimsy of a board game, as a throwback to the Saturday nights that Steph would spend with her brother and cousins playing Battleship and Monopoly. Whether you have time to make a Chinese checkers centerpiece or just a few seconds to print our ready-to-play boards, get set for some friendly (and tasty!) competition.

Materials:

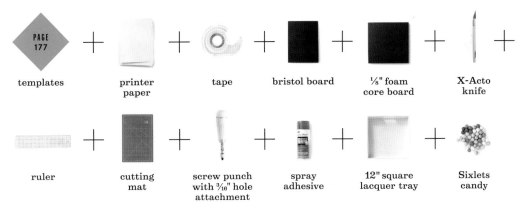

templates (PAGE 177)	printer paper	tape	bristol board	⅛" foam core board	X-Acto knife
ruler	cutting mat	screw punch with ³⁄₁₆" hole attachment	spray adhesive	12" square lacquer tray	Sixlets candy

MAKE THIS FOR → hostess gift | uncle's coffee table | cousin's dorm room

Steps:

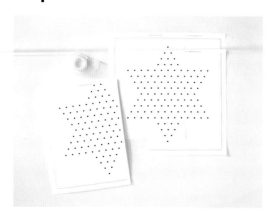

1. Print the templates onto paper and tile them together with tape. Trim the excess border along the lines.

2. Cut the bristol board and foam core board to 11½" × 11½".

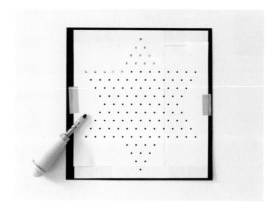

3. Center and tape the template to the bristol board. Punch holes according to the template.

4. Use spray adhesive to mount the bristol board to the foam core board and place them in the tray. To play, you will need six candy colors (we like using Sixlets) and ten pieces of each on the game board.

CAT AND MOUSE CHASE

It only takes a few minutes to assemble this game, our playful take on Chutes & Ladders. Print the templates (see page 178) onto cardstock and use double-stick tape to tile them together. You will need dice and some foil-wrapped chocolate mice to play.

↓

TIC-TAC-TOE— TO GO

This game board can be scaled to fit any square container. Simply print the template (see page 179) onto cardstock, trim to fit, and use any two types of candy. We prefer a lidded container so we can take our game anywhere!

start! →	1	2	3	Meow! Go back two squares.
9	Mouse trap! Sorry, go back to start.		6	5
10	Secret tunnel! Sneak down to #21.	12		14
19		17	Meow! Go back four squares.	Secret tunnel! Sneak down to #25.
20	21	22	23	
finish!	Meow! Go back eight squares.	27	Mouse trap! Sorry, go back to start.	25

Voracious Reader Tote

We designed this bag for our friends who are avid readers and always on the go: riding long stretches on the subway and bus, working and reading on their tablets, and catching up on current events. With individual pockets for a newspaper, iPad, iPhone, and subway card, all the essentials are easily at hand.

Materials:

3 18" × 18" felt squares	fabric scissors	48" of 1" wide cotton webbing	sewing pins	sewing machine	thread

MAKE THIS FOR → well-read husband | frequent traveller friend | multitasking sister

Steps:

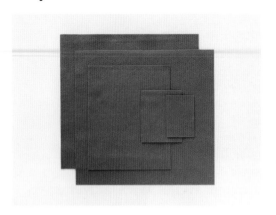

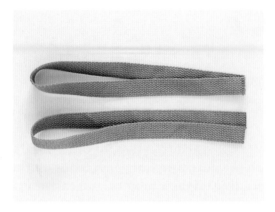

1. Cut felt to the following sizes: 2¾" × 4" (NYC subway card), 3½" × 5" (iPhone), 8¼" × 10" (iPad), and two pieces of 13" × 14" (*New York Times*).

2. Cut the webbing into two pieces that are 24" long.

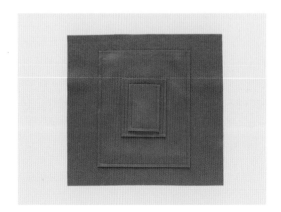

5. Pin the third felt in the center of the largest felt (just one of the pieces—this is the front of the tote) and sew along the sides and bottom with a ¼" seam.

6. Fold the webbing ends in by 1", and pin in place to the left and right of the largest pocket. Secure the webbing by sewing a square and an X on each end.

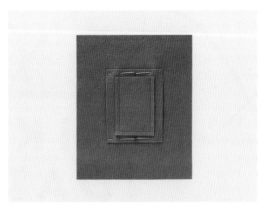

3. Pin the smallest felt in the center of the second smallest felt and sew along the sides and bottom with a ¼" seam.

4. Pin the second smallest felt in the center of the third felt and sew along the sides and bottom with a ¼" seam.

7. Sew the front and back together with a ¼" seam.

Tips:

Look for 100 percent wool felt, which is more durable than synthetic versions.

You can flip the front piece before sewing so the pockets face the inside of the tote.

Adjust the sizes of your pockets if you are holding different items in your tote, like your favorite book!

We prefer to use a sewing machine to save time and to ensure stitch strength, but you can also hand sew this project using a backstitch (see page 164).

Bike Dates

A bike ride is our favorite way to explore the city with the ones we love since it usually involves a reward at the end: a delicious meal, a fun neighborhood to discover, or a beautiful view. Use our templates to plan bike routes for a friend, with destinations suited to their interests. A set of customized itineraries, complete with a detachable bike bag to hold the essentials, offers the promise of a memorable day spent together.

Materials:

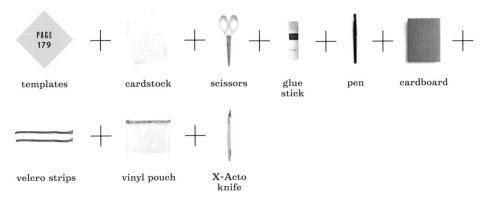

PAGE 179

templates + cardstock + scissors + glue stick + pen + cardboard +

velcro strips + vinyl pouch + X-Acto knife

| MAKE THIS FOR | → | first warm day of the year | playing hooky | Sunday morning family activity |

Steps:

1. Print templates onto cardstock and trim. (If necessary, scale templates to fit your pouch before printing.)

2. Use Google Maps to create a bike map for your destination. Print only the map portion, trim it to 7" wide by 4½" high, and glue it onto the map template.

3. Fill in the directions according to the mapped route.

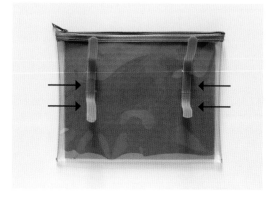

4. Cut two velcro straps to 6" lengths. Insert cardboard into the pouch, cut slits on the back side (see arrows), and thread velcro straps through the slits. Remove the cardboard and insert your custom maps.

BIKE DATES!

TO: Ole   FROM: Erin

DESTINATION: BROOKLYN FLEA

STARTING POINT

home

TOTAL TRAVEL TIME

30 min

1. Head east on 23rd St
2. Right onto 2nd Ave
3. Continue onto Chrystie St
4. Tu...
5. Le...
6. ...
7. Le...
8. Co...
9. ...
10. ...
11. _____
12. _____
13. _____

STARTING POINT: HOME   **DESTINATION:** BROOKLYN FLEA

Tip:

Of course, if you are in a hurry you can always print the map and directions as-is from Google Maps. Just package everything in the velcro pouch and head off on your adventure!

DESTINATION: NOGUCHI MUSEUM

STARTING POINT

home

TOTAL TRAVEL TIME

33 min

1. Head east on 23rd St
2. Left onto 1st Ave
3. Left onto E 59th St
4. Turn onto Queensboro Br
5. Right onto 21st St
6. Left at Queens Plaza N
7. R...
8. ...
9. ...
10. ...
11. _____
12. _____
13. _____
14. _____
15. _____
16. _____

STARTING POINT: HOME   **DESTINATION:** NOGUCHI MUSEUM

DESTINATION: ROBERTA'S PIZZA

STARTING POINT

home

TOTAL TRAVEL TIME

35 min

1. Head east on 23rd St
2. Right onto 2nd Ave
3. Left onto E 10th St
4. Right onto Avenue A
5. Left onto Stanton St
6. Right onto Suffolk St
7. Left onto Williamsburg Br
11. Right onto Marcy Ave
12. Left onto Rarington Pl
13. Right onto Humboldt St
14. Left onto Graham St
15. Left onto White St
16. Right onto Bocum St
17. Right onto Paroan St

STARTING POINT: HOME   **DESTINATION:** ROBERTA'S

Stockholm Utsikt från Söder med Stadshuset i bakgrunden

...adsvaart - P. Kooij, Rokin, Amsterdam

MISS YOU
GOOD LUCK
COME BACK
VISIT SOON
BOO-HOO

cheers!

Neon
Photo Postcards

We enjoy digging through old photos at home and finding unusual vintage postcards at flea markets. We also love screen printing, but not the work and cost that come with setting up a small print job. These postcards mimic the look with some basic office labels, tape, and a little inspiration from one of Erin's favorite artists, John Baldessari.

Materials:

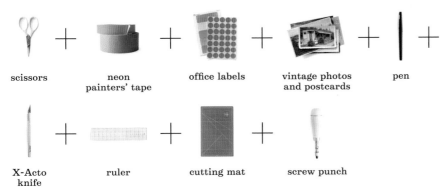

scissors   neon painters' tape   office labels   vintage photos and postcards   pen

X-Acto knife   ruler   cutting mat   screw punch

MAKE THIS FOR → pen pals | family reunion invitation | wedding save-the-dates

Steps:

1. Cut the tape and office labels into various shapes (see the chart below for our suggestions).
2. Add some flair to your photos and postcards.
3. Write a message on the back and send!

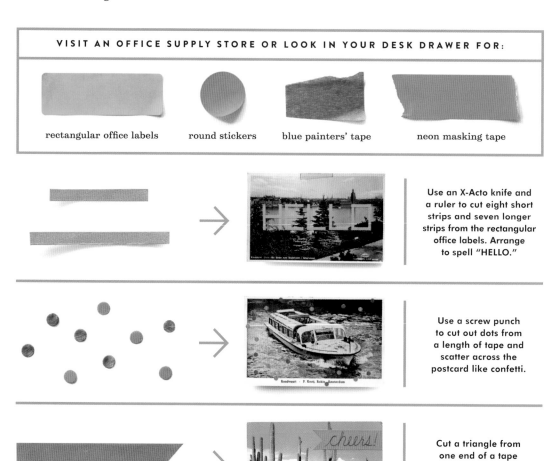

VISIT AN OFFICE SUPPLY STORE OR LOOK IN YOUR DESK DRAWER FOR:

rectangular office labels   round stickers   blue painters' tape   neon masking tape

Use an X-Acto knife and a ruler to cut eight short strips and seven longer strips from the rectangular office labels. Arrange to spell "HELLO."

Use a screw punch to cut out dots from a length of tape and scatter across the postcard like confetti.

Cut a triangle from one end of a tape strip, wrap around a postcard edge, and write a message.

Cut short strips of tape on the diagonal and space evenly around the border.

Cut long strips of tape to form an interesting border.

Cut a long triangle from an office label and form a speech bubble with a round sticker. Write captions.

Cut long triangles from an office label and place them around the subject like a sunburst.

Cut circle stickers in half, and adhere the half-moon shapes to the edge of your card, overlapping them slightly to create a scalloped edge.

Macaron Messages

Why wait until Valentine's Day to send a sweet message? Our twist on conversation heart candies, these colorful macarons are the perfect canvas for a handwritten sentiment. Romantic phrases in French pair perfectly with these Parisian treats, but sweet nothings in any language will do.

Materials:

templates (PAGE 181) + cardstock + scissors + X-Acto knife + ruler + cutting mat

bone folder + transparency paper + double-stick tape + macarons + food-safe markers

MAKE THIS FOR → date night | bridal shower | tea party

Steps:

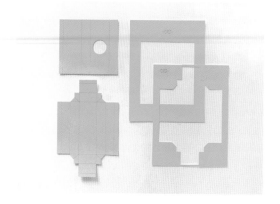

1. Print templates onto cardstock and cut them out.

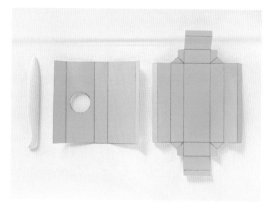

2. Score the box and the cover with the bone folder along the lines provided.

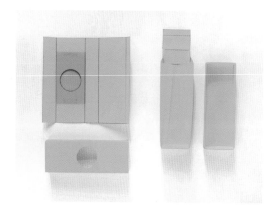

3. Cut the transparency to fit under the cover hole and tape to secure it. Assemble the cover and seal it with tape. Fold the interior box along the scored lines.

4. Write messages on the macarons. Allow them to dry completely before placing them in the sliding box.

LOVE NOTES (IN FRENCH!)

ma cherie	my darling
je t'aime	I love you
tu es mon soleil	you are my sunshine
bisou!	kiss!
mon amant	my lover
l'amour	love

Custom Growler

The guys in our lives are self-professed beer connoisseurs. They prefer specialty craft ales, so who better to give a customized growler that they can bring to their local brewer again and again—a vessel to hold their favorite "oat soda"?

Materials:

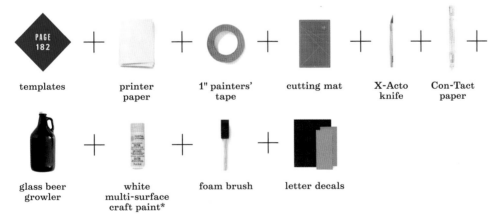

templates (PAGE 182)
+
printer paper
+
1" painters' tape
+
cutting mat
+
X-Acto knife
+
Con-Tact paper

glass beer growler
+
white multi-surface craft paint*
+
foam brush
+
letter decals

| MAKE THIS FOR → | first summer BBQ | boyfriend's poker night | beer-tasting party |

*We prefer this paint because it is opaque and will air cure on its own, but you can use real etching cream or glass paint if you prefer.

Steps:

1. Print templates onto paper.

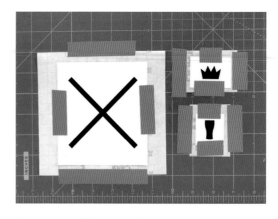

2. Cut around the X and icons, and tape them to the Con-Tact paper. Tape the Con-Tact paper to the cutting mat so it stays in place.

5. Apply paint to the growler using a foam brush and carefully peel off the Con-Tact paper while it is still wet to get a clean edge. Allow it to dry completely.

6. Adhere icon outlines to the growler. Paint icons and remove outlines while paint is still wet. Allow it to dry completely.

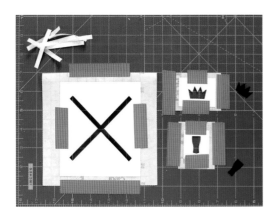

3. Cut out the X and icons carefully with an X-Acto knife. (You will be using the outlines as paint stencils.)

4. Adhere the X outline to the growler.

7. Adhere letter decal outlines to the growler. Paint letters and remove outlines while the paint is still wet. Allow it to dry completely.

8. Cure the paint according to the manufacturer's instructions.

James

Jimmy

JJ

Jimbo

Junior

Slim Jim

Nickname Handkerchiefs

Steph loves to come up with nicknames for her friends (E, Lizard, Jules, and Bri are just a few) as playful expressions of her affection for them. A pet name or term of endearment embroidered onto a hanky can become an instant keepsake for a lucky partner, friend, or family member. By giving a set of personalized pocket squares, we hope our loved ones will keep us close to their hearts (or at least think of us when they wipe their brow on a sunny day).

Materials:

handkerchiefs + water soluble marker + scissors + embroidery floss + sewing needle

---

MAKE THIS FOR → husband's suit | best friend's back pocket | grandma's cardigan

Steps:

1. Write a nickname on each handkerchief with the water-soluble marker.

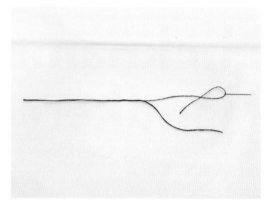

2. Cut 18" of floss. Separate two strands and thread your needle.

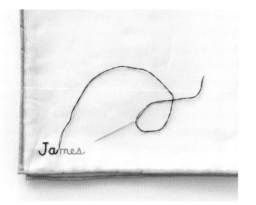

3. Embroider the name with backstitch (see page 164 for instructions). Knot and cut thread ends.

4. Blot the handkerchief with a wet towel to remove the ink.

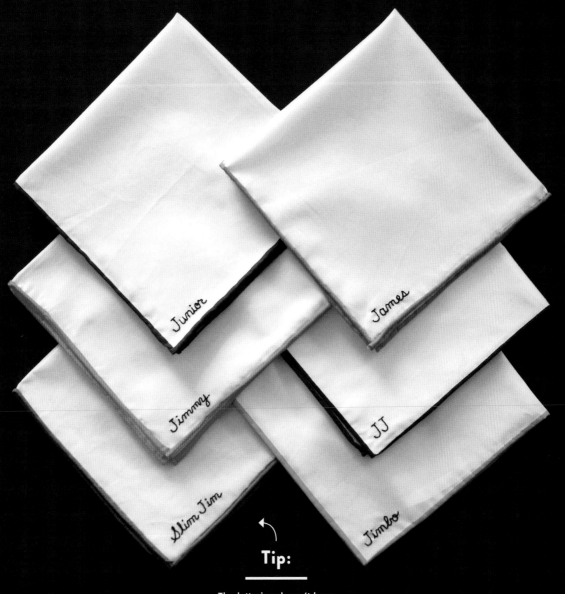

Junior

James

Jimmy

JJ

Slim Jim

Jimbo

Tip:

The lettering doesn't have
to be perfect. The closer it is to
your actual handwriting,
the more personal it becomes.

Trompe L'oeil Shoes

A tuxedo T-shirt makes us laugh because of its cheeky play on formalwear. With that in mind, we created these trompe l'oeil sneakers. Whether it's a beach day or a family night out, every child can put their best foot forward with these styles. They are simple to make, easy to wear, and most important, kid-approved. Our models even asked to take them home!

Materials:

PAGE 183	+		+		+		+		+	
templates		canvas shoes		iron-on transfer paper (for dark fabric)*		scissors		tea towels		iron

MAKE THIS FOR	→	wedding attire	rambunctious toddlers	last-minute costume

* Even though our shoes are white, we prefer the opacity and matte finish of iron-on transfers for dark fabrics. It is also the proper choice for any colored shoes.

Steps:

1. Measure the width of your shoe, and scale the templates to size (if necessary). Print the templates onto the transfer sheets.

2. Cut the templates out.

3. Roll up a tea towel and stuff it into a shoe so you have a firm ironing surface.

4. Heat-set the design with an iron according to the manufacturer's instructions. Allow it to dry completely before removing the tea towel. Use the tip of the iron for more control when heat-setting the rounded edges of the shoe.

Lavender Cloud Sachets

A rainy day or a quiet afternoon is perfect for making these felt clouds—
the scent of lavender is calming for both you and the one you give these to.
Steph likes to make these for friends, with hopes that if placed beneath
their pillows, her dearest will have sweet dreams.

Materials:

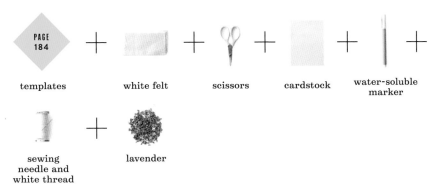

PAGE 184	white felt	scissors	cardstock	water-soluble marker
templates				

sewing
needle and
white thread

lavender

MAKE THIS FOR → grandma's linen drawer | baby's first mobile (attach the clouds to an embroidery hoop with string) | out-of-town guests

Steps:

1. Cut two 3" × 6" rectangles of felt and stack them together.

2. Print the template onto cardstock and cut out the cloud shape. Trace the cloud onto one layer of felt with a water-soluble marker.

4. Cut out the cloud.

5. Fill the sachet with lavender.

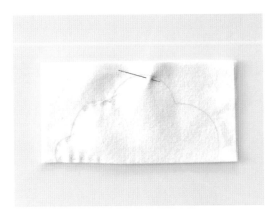

3. Sew through both layers of felt with a small running stitch (see page 164 for instructions) ⅛" inside the traced line, leaving a 2" gap along the bottom. Leave the needle and thread tail.

see page 164 for instructions

Tips:

Use thinner felt that is 2–3 mm thick—it is easier to sew, and the sachets will be more fragrant.

Dried herbs can be purchased in small quantities from stores that sell soap-making or herbalist supplies.

Try making clouds with other fillings such as cedar chips, rosemary, or chamomile.

A small paper bag stamped with "ZZZ . . ." makes the perfect packaging to wish someone a good night's rest.

6. Pick up the needle and sew the sachet closed. Knot and cut the thread.

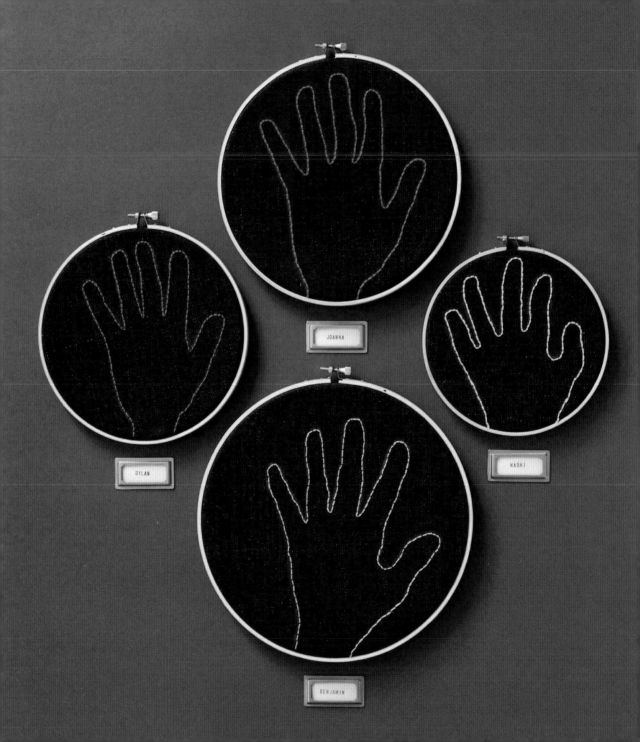

Family Tree Embroidery

Inspired by the ceramic keepsake prints parents traditionally make of their child's hand (Steph's mom still has hers after all these years!) —we wanted to create a sewn version of a family tree that can accommodate new members of the brood. Embroider each family member's handprint in their favorite color, and watch your gallery wall grow and change over the years.

Materials:

fabric + chalk + embroidery hoops + fabric scissors + sewing needle and embroidery floss

| MAKE THIS FOR → | family reunion | grandparents' gallery wall | wedding present |

Steps:

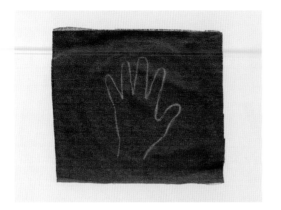

1. On a piece of fabric that is at least 2" larger than the hoop on all sides, trace your hand in the center with chalk. **TIP:** If you are using light-colored fabric you may prefer to use a water-soluble marker to trace the hands.

2. Stretch the fabric with an embroidery hoop, making sure it is taut.

3. Cut an 18" length of embroidery floss. Separate three of the six strands, and thread them through the needle. Sew the outline of your hand with a backstitch (see page 164 for instructions).

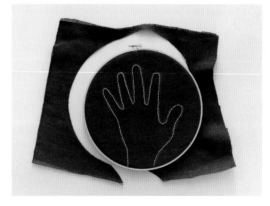

4. Cut away any excess fabric from the hoop.

NAOMI

DYLAN

JOANNA

BENJAMIN

Tip:
_____

Place adhesive nameplates
below your hung embroideries
for a polished look. We like
to think it makes them look like
modern art in a gallery.

Cake Portraits

Who wouldn't feel honored with a cake that bore their resemblance? Cake decorations are often made from fondant or inedible materials, so we prefer to buy or bake a plain frosted cake and render someone's likeness on it with candy. Try to capture at least one distinguishing feature about the person's face— like graying sideburns or freckles! Imitation is the sweetest form of flattery.

Materials:

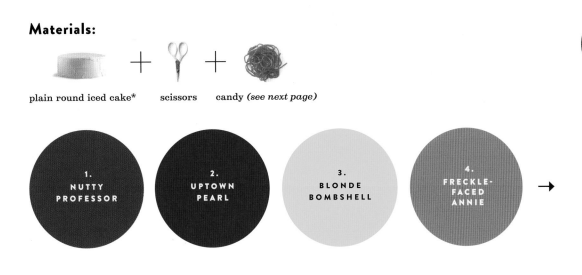

plain round iced cake*   scissors   candy *(see next page)*

1.
NUTTY
PROFESSOR

2.
UPTOWN
PEARL

3.
BLONDE
BOMBSHELL

4.
FRECKLE-
FACED
ANNIE

→

MAKE THIS FOR → guest of honor | retirement party | first pair of glasses

*Buy or frost a cake with colored or flavored icing if you want to capture someone's skin tone.

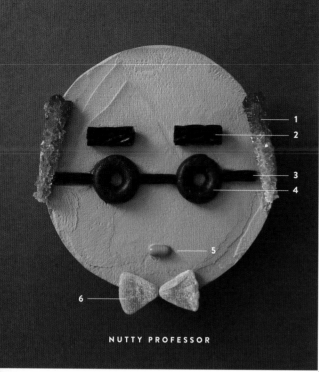

NUTTY PROFESSOR

1 **SIDEBURNS:** swizzle sticks with the wooden sticks trimmed off

2 **EYEBROWS:** thick licorice

3 **EYEGLASSES:** chocolate licorice

4 **EYEGLASS RIMS:** chocolate covered jelly rings

5 **MOUTH:** pink Good & Plenty

6 **BOW TIE:** sour grapefruit slices

1 **HAIR:** cotton candy*

2 **EYELASHES:** chocolate-covered sunflower seeds

3 **EYES:** blue M&Ms

4 **MOLE:** chocolate pearl

5 **LIPS:** foil-wrapped chocolate heart

6 **NECKLACE:** rock candy

*Tear it off in large pieces and handle it as little as possible to preserve its fluffy texture.

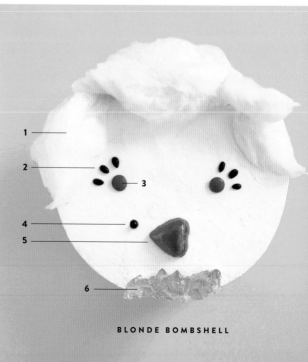

BLONDE BOMBSHELL

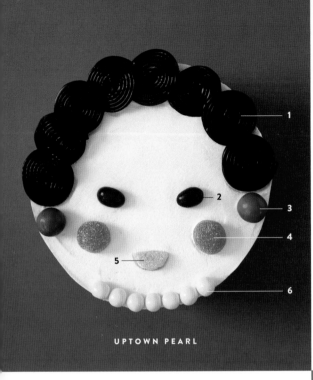

UPTOWN PEARL

① **HAIR:**
black licorice wheels

② **EYES:**
chocolate covered almonds

③ **EARRINGS:**
large gumballs

④ **CHEEKS:**
large gumdrops

⑤ **LIPS:**
sour watermelon slice

⑥ **PEARLS:**
small white gumballs

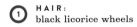

① **HAIR:**
red licorice laces (braided!)

② **BANGS:**
watermelon jelly
fruit slices

③ **EYES:**
blackberry gummy candies

④ **EYEBROWS:**
licorice pastilles

⑤ **FRECKLES:**
yellow Nerds

⑥ **MOUTH:**
cherry jelly slice

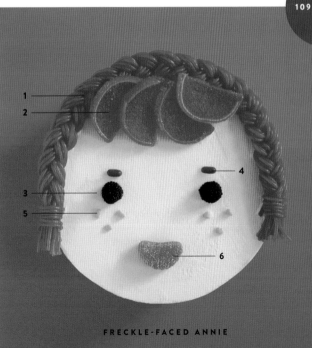

FRECKLE-FACED ANNIE

Rebus Wall Hanging

We love a rebus puzzle. The fun is in decoding the hidden message in the mix of letters and symbols. Images from vintage decoupage books and clip art etchings feel modern when paired with geometric honeycomb shapes and neon twine. Draw your own coded message onto punched circles, or use our templates. We strung this affectionate saying ("I love you always") into a mobile that doubles as wall art.

Materials:

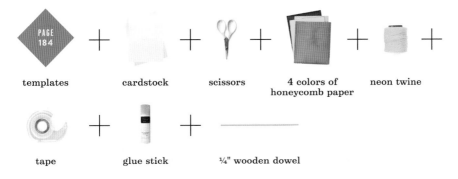

PAGE 184	+		+		+		+		+	
templates		cardstock		scissors		4 colors of honeycomb paper		neon twine		

	+		+	
tape		glue stick		¼" wooden dowel

MAKE THIS FOR	→	baby nursery	creative office decor	kid's reading room

Steps:

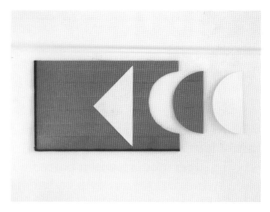

1. Print the rebus templates onto cardstock and cut them out.

2. Print the diamond and circle templates onto cardstock and cut them out. Lay the half-diamond and half-circle templates onto the honeycomb paper and cut them out.

5. Lay the rebus icons and honeycomb shapes 2" apart along the twine, and secure with tape on the back.

6. Trim the string ends.

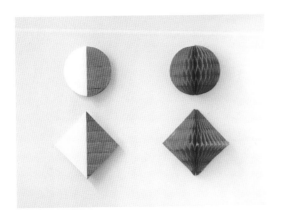

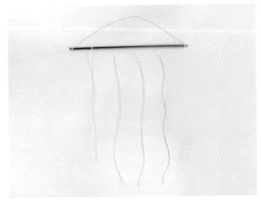

3. Open the honeycomb shapes and glue them to the full diamond and full circle cardstock templates. Repeat for the three remaining honeycomb colors.

4. Trim the wood dowel to 20" Cut a 24" strand of twine and tie it to both ends of the dowel—this will become the hanging string. Cut four 20" strands of twine and tie them to the dowel so they hang vertically. Space the strings evenly across the dowel.

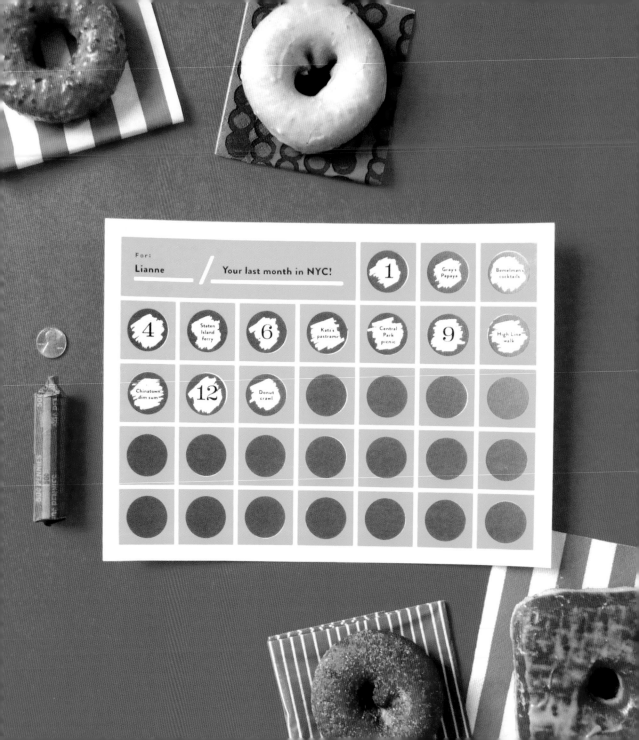

Scratch-Off Calendar

There's something irresistible about scratch-off tickets. The allure of winning a prize or discovering a secret message is pure fun. Combined with the thrill of a countdown, these calendars make the most of passing time. When friends told us of their impending move out of the city, we created this "NYC Bucket List" to help them leave with no regrets. Use the blank calendar template to customize your own, and surprise someone with a lineup of activities to look forward to all month.

Materials:

PAGE 185 templates

+

cardstock

+

label paper

+

1" circle punch

+

marker

+

1" round scratch-off labels

| **MAKE THIS FOR** → | last month of summer break | mom-to-be's final days of pregnancy | FOMO (Fear of Missing Out) action plan |

Steps:

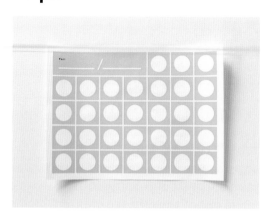

1. Print the calendar template onto cardstock.

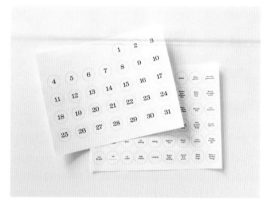

2. Print activities and numbers templates onto label paper.

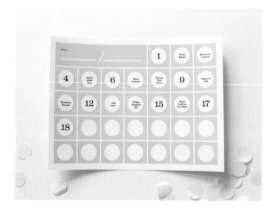

4. Adhere the labels onto the blank circles of the template, filling in the days with activities or numbers.

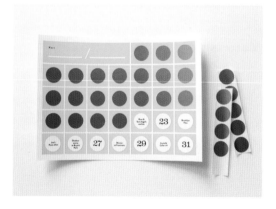

5. Cover activities and numbers with scratch-off labels.

3. Use a circle punch to cut out the activities and numbers.

Tips:

Our "NYC Bucket List" (see page 186 for the template) is a surefire way to make anyone stay, move to, or fall in love with the city!

Customize your calendar with our activity suggestions, or simply fill in the blanks with your own handwritten ideas.

6. Fill in the name and occasion blanks on the calendar.

People help each other

Hand-Drawn Pillows

Picasso said, "It took me four years to paint like Raphael, but a lifetime to paint like a child." As all parents know, every kid's drawing is a masterpiece. Doodles and artwork quickly scribbled onto scraps of paper are often the most special to us, because they capture a little one's carefree spirit. Any child would be thrilled to receive a keepsake of their own design, so we made pillows with custom fabric made from their drawings. Like a snapshot in time, these soft goods will surely be cherished for years to come.

Materials:

| drawings | fabric scissors | sewing machine | sewing needle and thread | pillow stuffing |

MAKE THIS FOR → nephew's naptime | grandma's favorite chair | teacher appreciation

Steps:

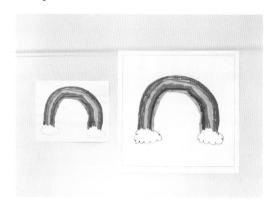

1. Scan drawings* into a computer design program like Photoshop. Add at least a 2" margin around your design (so the image isn't lost when the pillow is stuffed)—this will be your cut line. Don't forget to order enough fabric for the back of each pillow. Order Spoonflower fabric according to their instructions online. We use heavy cotton twill for throw cushions.

2. Cut out the pillow pieces. With right sides facing, sew the front and back together with a ½" seam allowance. Leave a 5" opening.

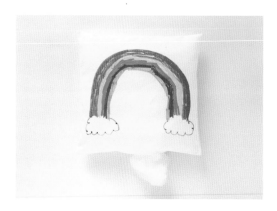

5. Fill the pillow with stuffing.

6. Hand sew the pillow closed with a whipstitch (see page 164 for instructions).

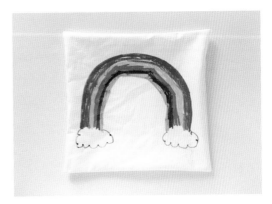

3. Trim corners close to the seam (for sharp points) and notch all curves (for any rounded designs like our heart pillow).

4. Turn the pillow right side out.

* We scan our images at 300 dpi resolution at 100 percent, but you should increase the size percentage if enlarging a small drawing for a larger pillow.

DIRT CANDY
rhubarb

D🍩NUTS

strawberries

blueberries

cameo

mutsu

cortland

honeycrisp

Farmers' Market Gifts

We grew up with mothers who like to bring fruit to a party—it's fresh, easy to share, and everyone can appreciate nature's bounty. Now that we both live near farmers' markets, we've adopted our mothers' tradition because there is something special about scoring the season's best. Our playful packaging ideas go a step further to turn simple produce into gifts to please any host.

A few of our favorite things (and when to find them!):

1. DIRT CANDY
(asparagus/ rhubarb)
—
spring

2. DONUT PEACHES
—
late spring or summer

3. BERRY PIE
(strawberries/ blueberries)
—
summer

4. APPLE SAMPLER
—
fall

MAKE THIS FOR → get-well visit | potluck | picnic in the park

DIRT CANDY

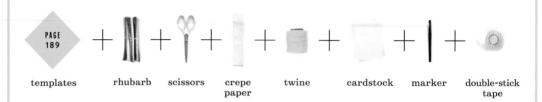

1. Trim the rhubarb to the same height and bundle to 3½" diameter.
2. Roll the rhubarb in crepe paper three times and tie the ends with twine.
3. Print the template onto cardstock and write the produce name.
4. Wrap cardstock around the rhubarb and secure with double-stick tape.

BERRY PIE

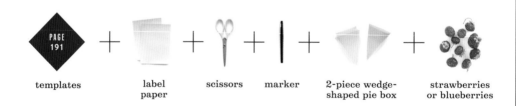

1. Print the template onto label paper and cut out the pie slice.
2. Write the berry type on the crust part of the template.
3. Adhere the label to the box lid.
4. Place the berries in the box and close it with the lid.

DONUT PEACHES

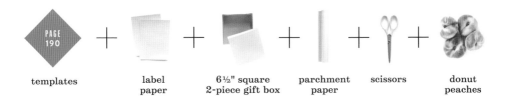

templates	label paper	6½" square 2-piece gift box	parchment paper	scissors	donut peaches

1. Print the template onto label paper.
2. Adhere the label to the box lid.
3. Cut parchment paper to fit the box with a 4" overhang on both sides, place donut peaches in the box, and fold in the parchment paper.
4. Close the donut box.

APPLE SAMPLER

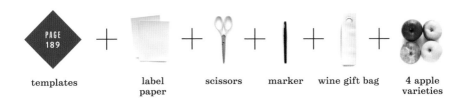

templates	label paper	scissors	marker	wine gift bag	4 apple varieties

1. Print the template onto the label paper and cut out the circles.
2. Write the apple varieties on the labels.
3. Adhere labels to the front of the bag.
4. Stack apples in the bag to match the order of the labels.

YEAR BOOK

Trips to
Greece + Paris

YEAR BOOK

Miles
Age 1

Yearbook Photo Album

We take and store so many photos on our camera phones, but there's nothing like flipping through a physical album. Our version of a "brag book," these little albums are the perfect size for carrying and passing around. We love that these CD sleeves have pre-cut circles that are just right for framing photos from trips and everyday moments of family and friends. We like to include twelve photos in each book as a "year in review" theme, but you can add as many photos as you like.

Materials:

templates + printer paper + **13 CD paper sleeves** *(or 12 if you prefer to use a photo as the cover)* + **12 square photos,** printed to 4¾" × 4¾" size + screw punch + split pins + marker

PAGE 192

MAKE THIS FOR → family vacation | senior year of high school | baby's first year

Steps:

1. Print the templates onto paper and cut them out. Fold the binding template along the dotted line.

2. Print the photos and trim them to 4¾" × 4¾".

5. Insert photos into the sleeves.

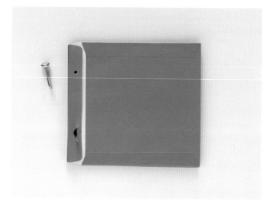

6. Stack the sleeves together and insert split pins from the front. Separate the ends in the back.

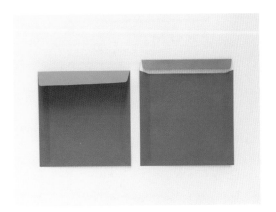

3. Fold the sleeve tab in half. Repeat for all CD sleeves.

4. Place the folded binding template over one folded sleeve tab. Line up the edges and punch holes. Repeat for all CD sleeves.

7. Fill in the cover template and place it into the front paper sleeve.

8. Use our cover template or a photo as the album cover.

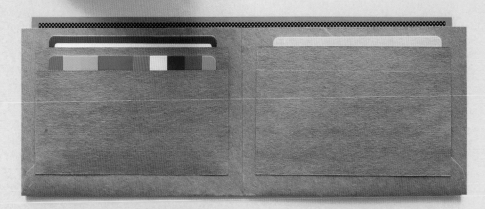

Thanks for showing me all your favorite **FOR YOU!** local spots— I had so much fun together!

Thank-You Wallet

Finding the perfect thank-you gift is a tall order, but it's easy to take note of the things someone likes. We've found that hosts always take us to their favorite spots when we visit, so why not purchase small gift cards along the way (discreetly, of course)? Nominal amounts for a cup of their daily coffee, a magazine from their local bookstore, or a pastry from "the best" bakery can be just enough to make their day.

Materials:

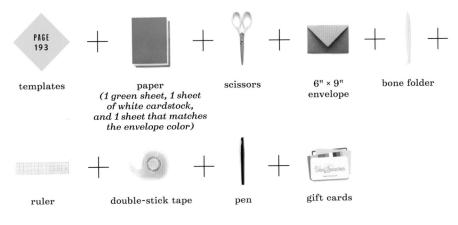

PAGE 193	**paper** *(1 green sheet, 1 sheet of white cardstock, and 1 sheet that matches the envelope color)*	**scissors**	**6" × 9" envelope**	**bone folder**
templates				

ruler	**double-stick tape**	**pen**	**gift cards**

MAKE THIS FOR →	vacation at aunt's pied-a-terre	weekend at boyfriend's parents' house	visit to niece's college town

Steps:

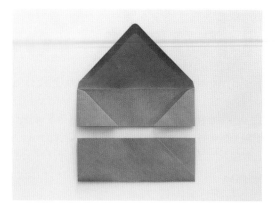

1. Print the thank-you card templates onto white cardstock and the money template on green paper. Cut them out.

2. Trim the envelope to 3 ¼" height on the open side.

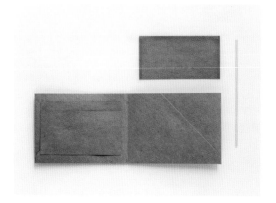

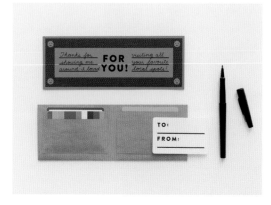

5. Cut ⅛" strips of double-stick tape and adhere to the sides and bottom of the wallet pockets. Attach two pockets to each side of the wallet.

6. Fill the pockets with gift cards. Write a note on the green paper and place in the wallet.

3. Crease the envelope in half with the bone folder and ruler.

4. Cut four 2" × 3⅞" rectangles of paper. These will be the wallet pockets.

Pressed Herb Prints

Our love for pressed plants and flowers inspired us to put all the leftover herbs in our fridge to good use. With the help of some heavy books and a little patience, we shaped our pressed herbs into framed art that will brighten up any kitchen. Take advantage of the different textures and shapes of each herb. We think rosemary works best for straight letters, while oregano and thyme are ideal for curved lines.

Materials:

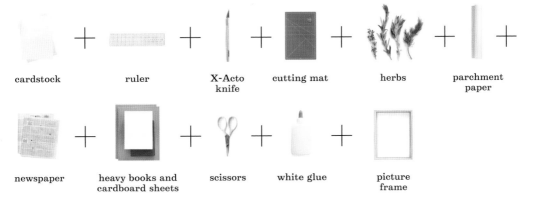

cardstock   ruler   X-Acto knife   cutting mat   herbs   parchment paper

newspaper   heavy books and cardboard sheets   scissors   white glue   picture frame

MAKE THIS FOR → foodie friend | grandpa with a green thumb | community garden neighbor

Steps:

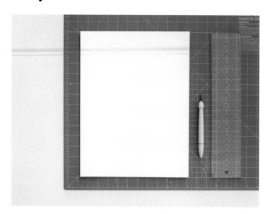

1. Trim the cardstock to the dimensions of your picture frame using an X-Acto knife, ruler, and cutting mat.

2. Cut the herbs into small sprigs and lay them onto one side of a sheet of folded parchment paper.

5. Arrange the pressed herbs in the shape of your desired letters. Trim stems and unwanted pieces with scissors. Secure the herbs to the cardstock with a dab of glue. Allow them to dry completely.

6. Frame the pressed herbs.

3. Fold the parchment paper over and sandwich it between newspaper and two cardboard sheets.

4. Place heavy books on top of the cardboard stack. Allow the herbs to dry and press flat for seven to ten days.

PARTY ANIMAL

LAURA ADLER
212 673 8455

Unofficial Business Cards

We made these business cards to acknowledge the incredible talents and big personalities of the people we love—the nephew who thinks he's a superhero, the grandma whose green thumb grows the best zucchini every year, or the fabulous friend who is a karaoke queen. We love that these calling cards offer more humor and personality than just a name and a number. With bright colors and funny titles, these cards will let their recipients know that we think they are officially awesome.

Materials:

stamp set   +   black or white ink pad   +   blank business cards

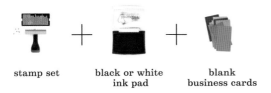

MAKE THIS FOR → coworker crush | college graduation | bachelorette party

Steps:

1. Set the letters into the stamp block. (Remember to spell your title backward.)
2. Stamp the title onto the business card. Allow it to dry.

3. Reset the stamp block with letters and numbers.
4. Stamp contact information onto the reverse side of each business card.

HERE ARE SOME FUN SUGGESTIONS!

WINNER

BIG KAHUNA

GENIUS

MAESTRO

THE BOSS

SWEETHEART

GRAND POOBAH

THE MAN

DUDE

GREEN THUMB

TOP DOG

FUN EXPERT

NUTTY PROFESSOR	NO.1	CHAMPION
MASTER ★ COMMANDER	SUPERWOMAN	ADVENTURER
PROFESSIONAL WANDERER	HOT SHOT	DANCING QUEEN
SUPERSTAR	DIVA	GODDESS
VIP	JACK OF ALL TRADES	CAPTAIN

Day & Night Clock Face

As a curious toddler with boundless energy, Erin's son would stay up all night if he could. We originally designed this clock for little ones like him, who sometimes need a gentle reminder that it's time for bed, but it also makes a whimsical gift for grownups: a sunny face to help them rise and shine in the morning, and a sleepy face to wish them a good night.

Materials:

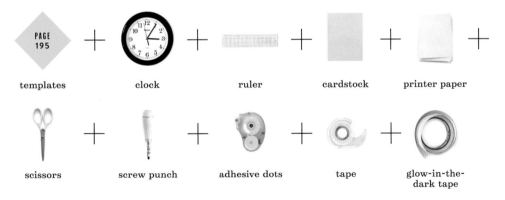

PAGE 195	clock	ruler	cardstock	printer paper
templates				

scissors	screw punch	adhesive dots	tape	glow-in-the-dark tape

MAKE THIS FOR → kid's bedroom | neighbor's kitchen | cousin's dorm room

Steps:

1. Disassemble the clock, and measure the diameter of the clock face.

2. Scale the templates to size. Print the clock face onto the cardstock and the tape templates onto the printer paper.

5. Adhere the glow-in-the-dark eyes and mouth to the cardstock face.

6. Reassemble the clock.

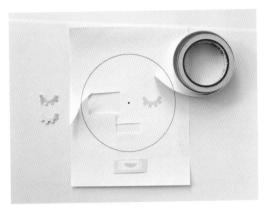

3. Cut out the face and and make the center hole with a screw punch. Attach the face to the clock with adhesive dots.

4. Tape the eye and mouth templates to the glow-in-the-dark tape and cut them out.

Tips:

Match the cardstock to the color of the glow-in-the-dark tape so the tape blends in with the clock face.

We purchased glow-in-the-dark tape with a peel-off backing to make it easier to handle.

LOVE

AWESOME

ME&YOU

Accordion Cards

Die-cut cards are impressive but can be expensive to order from a printer. We wanted to create a similar look using these affordable letter stencils that can be found in most art and hardware stores. Erin loves incorporating interesting folds in her paper designs, so we taped these stencils together to make simple accordion cards. Painting the letters in bright colors makes them pop, and customized expressions make a statement worth keeping and displaying on a shelf.

Materials:

letter stencils + gouache paint + paint pouncer + tape + scissors

MAKE THIS FOR → job promotion | new baby | welcome home

Steps:

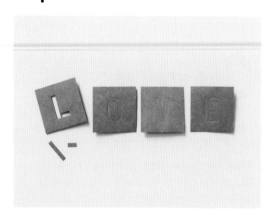

1. Choose a word or phrase for the card. Select your letters and separate them from the stencils.

2. Use the pouncer to apply a thin and even coat of gouache onto the stencils. Allow them to dry completely.

Tips:

You can also use spray paint—be sure to apply thin coats to avoid drips or soaking the stencils.

We like to use gouache because it is thick, opaque, and comes in the brightest colors in our art store.

If the stencils are curled after drying, flatten them between a heavy book before taping them together.

4. Trim the tape ends with scissors.

3. Tape the letters together on the back side.

5. Reinforce the folds with your fingers or a bone folder (if necessary).

Here are some suggestions for phrases that use only one or two packs of letter stencils

↓

CONGRATS

BABY

SWEET16

HERO

SORRY

STUD

HELLO

FAREWELL

DUDE

FANCY

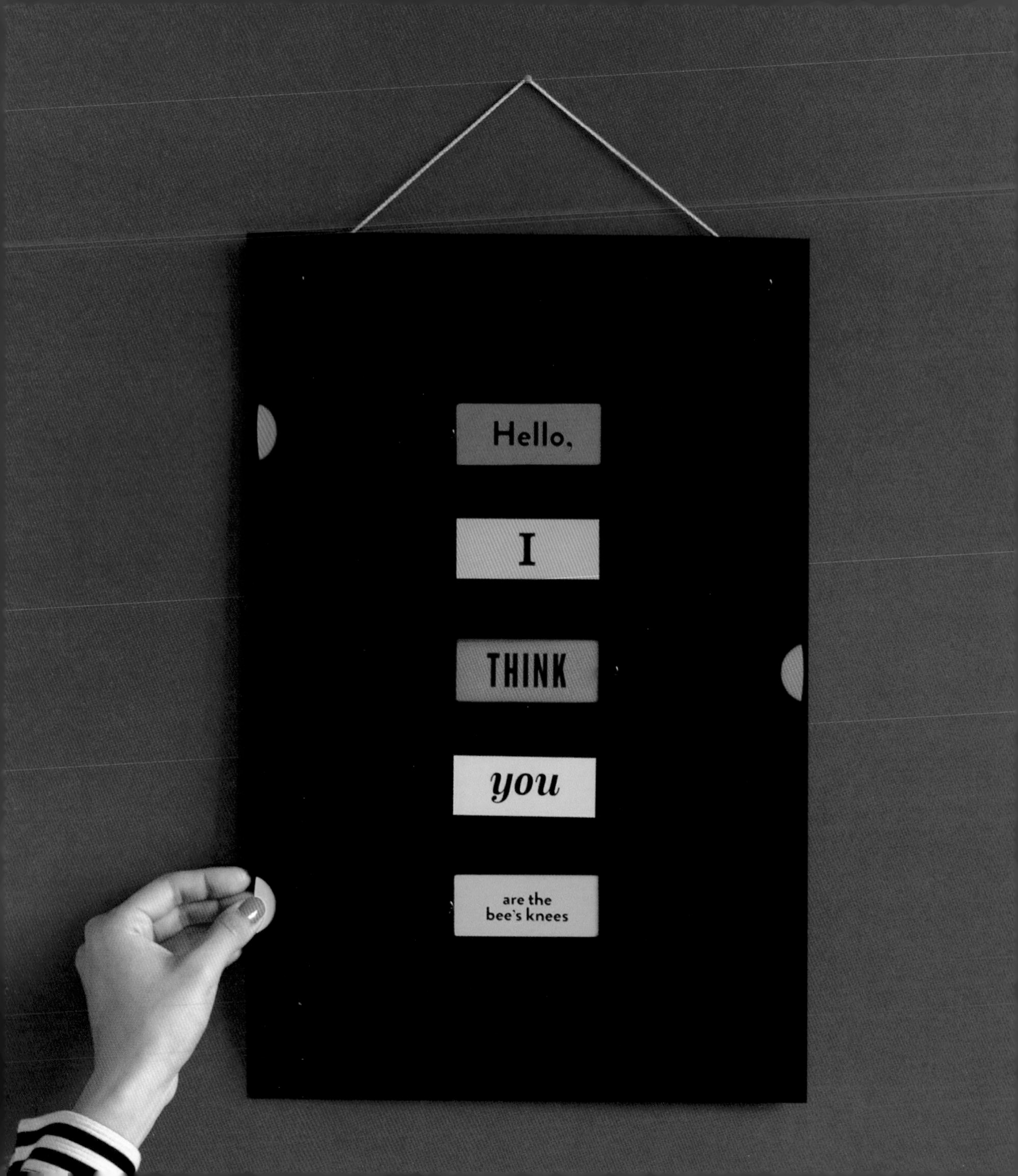
Hello,
I
THINK
you
are the
bee's knees

Perpetual Greeting

Erin is a night owl, but her husband, Abe, is often out the door before the sun is up. Different work or sleep schedules can sometimes mean missing your loved ones even when you live under the same roof—like passing ships in the night. We created this oversized greeting card so you can leave each other messages even if you are always rushing out the door. It also ensures that you will always find the right words.

Materials:

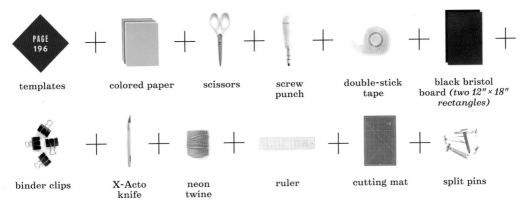

PAGE 196	colored paper	scissors	screw punch	double-stick tape	black bristol board *(two 12" × 18" rectangles)*
templates					

binder clips	X-Acto knife	neon twine	ruler	cutting mat	split pins

MAKE THIS FOR → roommate | day shift / night shift couple | sweetheart

Steps:

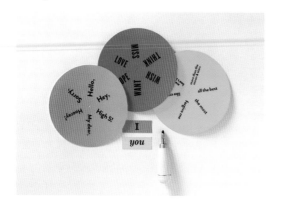

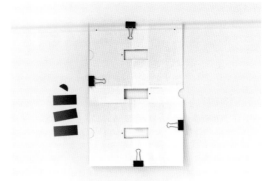

1. Print the disc and rectangle templates onto colored paper and cut them out. Make a small hole in the center of each disc using a screw punch.

2. Tile the cover templates with double-stick tape and trim off the excess border. Lay the template over one piece of bristol board and secure with binder clips. Cut out the rectangles and semicircles using an X-Acto knife, ruler, and cutting mat—this will be the front piece. Unclip and add the second bristol board to the back of the stack. Secure with binder clips again and punch holes in both bristol boards according to the template.

SPIN A SALUTATION

There is a variety of different phrases you can construct with our perpetual greeting. Here are a few favorite messages you can make, but turn the wheels and make up your own!

→

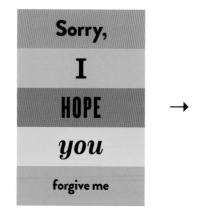

→

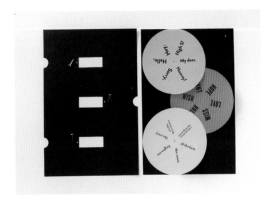

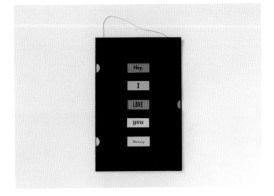

3. Layer the discs in between the bristol boards, lining up the holes.

4. Secure the layers with split pins and tape "I" and "You" onto the cover, spaced evenly between the cutout rectangles. Place split pins in the top corner holes of the bristol boards, then push them through the knotted ends of a piece of twine (this will become your hanging string). **TIP**: Color the tops of the split pins with a black permanent marker.

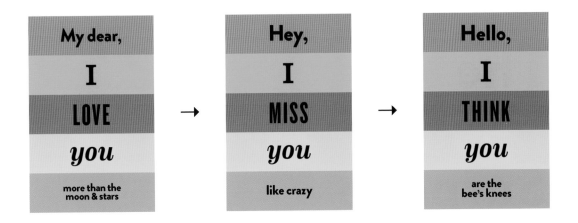

154

The Ultimate Desk Surprise

Projects:

1. NEON ACCENT
2. STATEMENT WALL
3. COFFEE BREAK
4. SUNNY CITRUS
5. WELCOME SCREEN
6. FRESH CUP
7. TEXT MESSAGE
8. MOUSE TRAP
9. SNACK ATTACK

①
②
③
⑤
⑥
after!
Hey, Sunshine!
④
⑧
⑨
⑦

When we both worked at *Martha Stewart Living* we saw so many creative ways in which coworkers surprised each other. Whether it was a practical joke, birthday gift, or a last-day farewell, the recipient was always smiling when they arrived at their desk. We combined our favorite ideas for one giant *"ta-da!"* but even one or two will create a memorable moment.

MAKE THIS FOR ⟶ coworker send-off | freelancer beau | housemate

Projects:

① **NEON ACCENT** Swap out white printer paper for a stack of neon paper to brighten up those dull office memos!

② **STATEMENT WALL** One pack of sticky notes will instantly transform a plain cubicle wall. Choose a bright color (We love these neon circular ones!) and overlap them slightly to create a scalloped effect. Take it one step further and write secret messages behind a few of the notes.

③ **COFFEE BREAK** We love our afternoon coffee and sweet treat. Make someone's day by leaving a pastry on their desk with a custom cake topper. Tuck a small bill into a mini envelope (enough money to indulge in their favorite latte), along with a handwritten note, and tape it to a toothpick.

④ **SUNNY CITRUS** Adhesive googly eyes and a winning smile give this fruit an easy upgrade.

⑤

WELCOME SCREEN Hijack the computer by uploading our image (see page 201 for the template) as the desktop screensaver. A shock of color and happy greeting will be a welcome sight for anyone returning to their desk.

⑥

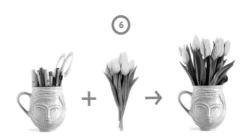

FRESH CUP Stash the pens and fill a cup with fresh blooms for a burst of sunshine.

⑦

TEXT MESSAGE Use a scratchpad or memo book (there is always one on the desk!) and write a heartfelt note from yours truly.

⑧

MOUSE TRAP This trick is borrowed from a former coworker and office prankster, who pulled a fast one on April Fool's Day. A cleverly placed note is all it takes to create some minor office mischief.

⑨

SNACK ATTACK A simple switch of desk accessories for tasty snacks will curb any hunger pangs.

HONEY

SO YOUR LIFE
WILL ALWAYS
BE SWEET

WINE

SO YOU WILL ALWAYS
BE FULL OF GOOD CH...

SALT

SO YOUR LIFE
WILL ALWAYS
BE FULL OF
FLAVOR

OLIVE OIL

SO YOU WILL
ALWAYS
LIVE IN GOOD
HEALTH

BREAD

BELLY WILL ALWAYS
BE FULL
SO YOUR

BRUSH

SO YOU CAN
SWEEP ALL YOUR
TROUBLES AWAY

Essential Housewarming Gift Guide

When we saw these simple gabled cardboard boxes, the shape reminded us so much of a real house that we were inspired to create a modern package for our favorite, classic housewarming gifts. Use our label templates to decorate your "house" and fill it with meaningful and practical gifts, an offering of happiness and prosperity in a new home.

Materials:

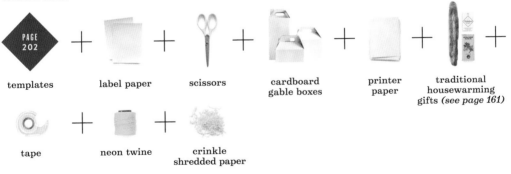

PAGE 202	+ label paper	+ scissors	+ cardboard gable boxes	+ printer paper	+ traditional housewarming gifts *(see page 161)*
templates					

tape	+ neon twine	+ crinkle shredded paper

MAKE THIS FOR → couple moving in together | first-time homeowner | niece's off-campus house

Steps:

1. Print the house templates onto label paper.

2. Cut out the house templates and adhere them to the assembled box.

3. Print the gift labels onto paper. Cut them out and wrap them around the items, securing them with tape or twine.

4. Fill the box with crinkle shredded paper and gift items.

FULL HOUSE

Here are some of our favorite housewarming gifts. Choose the ones you feel would be most appropriate for the recipient, or select items that will fit nicely in your box.

→

OLIVE OIL

SO YOU WILL ALWAYS LIVE IN GOOD HEALTH

HONEY

SO YOUR LIFE WILL ALWAYS BE SWEET

CANDLE
TO YOU WILL ALWAYS HAVE LIGHT

WOOD

SO YOUR HOME WILL ALWAYS HAVE STABILITY

SALT

SO YOUR LIFE

WILL ALWAYS

BE FULL OF

FLAVOR

BRUSH
SO YOU WILL ALWAYS MAKE CLEAN START AWAY

BREAD

SO YOUR BELLY WILL ALWAYS BE FULL

WINE

SO YOU WILL ALWAYS BE FULL OF GOOD CHEER

SOURCES BY PROJECT

Candy Capsule Necklaces PAGE 23
· vending capsules (www.heyyoyo.com)
· rattail cord (www.mjtrim.com)

Fill-in-the-Blank Tattoos PAGE 39
· tattoo paper (www.decalpaper.com)

Everyday Advent PAGE 43
· large pillbox (www.amazon.com)

Secret Love Note Shirt PAGE 47
· iron-on transfer paper (www.amazon.com)

Personal Storybook PAGE 51
· blank board book (www.amazon.com)

Tea Sampler PAGE 59
· petri dishes (www.mcphee.com)

Candy Board Games PAGE 67
· square lacquer tray (www.westelm.com)
· chocolate mice (www.economycandy.com)
· bulk Sixlets (www.economycandy.com)

Voracious Reader Tote PAGE 71
· 18" × 18" felt squares (www.purlsoho.com)
· 1" cotton webbing (www.purlsoho.com)

Bike Dates PAGE 75
· vinyl pouch (www.muji.us)
· velcro straps (www.homedepot.com)

Neon Photo Postcards PAGE 79
· vintage postcards (www.brooklynflea.com)

Macaron Messages PAGE 83
· food-safe markers (www.whisknyc.com)

Custom Growler PAGE 87
· glass beer growler (www.amazon.com)

Nickname Handkerchiefs PAGE 91
· edged handkerchiefs (www.thetiebar.com)
· water-soluble marker (www.amazon.com)

Trompe L'oeil Shoes PAGE 95
· iron-on transfer paper (for dark fabric)
  (www.amazon.com)
· heart-printed leggings on model
  (www.houseofmia.com)

Lavender Cloud Sachets PAGE 99
· lavender (www.flowerpower.net)

Family Tree Embroidery PAGE 103
· embroidery floss (www.purlsoho.com)

Rebus Wall Hanging PAGE 111
· honeycomb paper (www.devra-party.com)

Scratch-Off Calendar PAGE 115
· 1" round scratch-off labels
  (www.myscratchofflabels.com)

Hand-Drawn Pillows PAGE 119
- custom-printed fabric (www.spoonflower.com)

Farmers' Market Gifts PAGE 123
- wine bag with handle (www.jampaper.com)
- pie box (www.etsy.com/ca/shop/alamodo)

Yearbook Photo Album PAGE 127
- CD paper sleeves (www.amazon.com)

Unofficial Business Cards PAGE 139
- blank business cards (www.paperpresentation.com)
- stamp set (www.staples.com)

Day & Night Clock Face PAGE 143
- glow-in-the-dark tape (www.setshop.com)

Accordion Cards PAGE 147
- letter stencils (www.homedepot.com)

The Ultimate Desk Surprise PAGE 154
- paper & accessories trays (www.poppin.com)
- round sticky notes (www.saturday.com)
- chocolate bars (www.chocolate-editions.com)

Essential Housewarming Gift Guide PAGE 159
- cardboard gable boxes (www.containerstore.com)
- crinkle shredded paper (www.paperpresentation.com)

RESOURCES

General Crafts
DICK BLICK: www.dickblick.com
MARTHA STEWART CRAFTS:
   shop.marthastewart.com
MICHAELS: www.michaels.com
MUJI: www.muji.us
HOME DEPOT: www.homedepot.com
AMAZON: www.amazon.com

Jewelry
M&J TRIMMING: www.mjtrim.com

Office
POPPIN: www.poppin.com
STAPLES: www.staples.com
KATE SPADE SATURDAY:
   www.saturday.com

Sewing
PURL SOHO: www.purlsoho.com
SPOONFLOWER: www.spoonflower.com

Home
WILLIAMS-SONOMA:
   www.williams-sonoma.com
WEST ELM: www.westelm.com
THE CONTAINER STORE:
   www.containerstore.com

Food
ECONOMY CANDY:
   www.economycandy.com

163

DYLAN'S CANDY BAR:
www.dylanscandybar.com
NY CAKE AND BAKING DIST.:
www.nycake.com
STEPHMODO: www.stephmodo.com
CHOCOLATE EDITIONS:
www.chocolate-editions.com

Paper

PAPER PRESENTATION:
www.paperpresentation.com
JAM PAPER: www.jampaper.com
PAPER SOURCE: www.paper-source.com

Toys, Specialty, and Other Fun Things

BROOKLYN FLEA: www.brooklynflea.com
ARCHIE MCPHEES: www.mcphee.com
TATTLY: www.tattly.com
KNOT AND BOW: www.knotandbow.com
HOUSE OF MIA: www.houseofmia.com
HEY YO YO: www.heyyoyo.com

STITCHING TECHNIQUES

Weave a length of thread through the eye of a hand sewing needle. Pull the needle halfway down the length of thread, fold the thread in half, and knots its ends together. Insert the needle into the fabric and pull gently until you feel the resistance of the knot. Using the diagrams below, make small even stitches with the needle according to the numbers provided. After the last stitch, knot the thread again and cut off the excess.

Running Stitch
(Lavender Cloud Sachets)

Backstitch
(Family Tree Embroidery, Nickname Handkerchiefs)

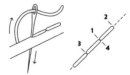

Whipstitch
(Hand-Drawn Pillows)

Templates

All of the templates and clip art for the projects in this book can be found on the following pages. Unless directed otherwise, copy the templates at 100 percent, or size to your project as needed.

165

PDF files of these templates are also available to download at www.roostbooks.com/makeandgive. Please use the templates from this book for your own personal use.

Flower Pun Bouquets

PAGE 31, ENLARGE TO 165%

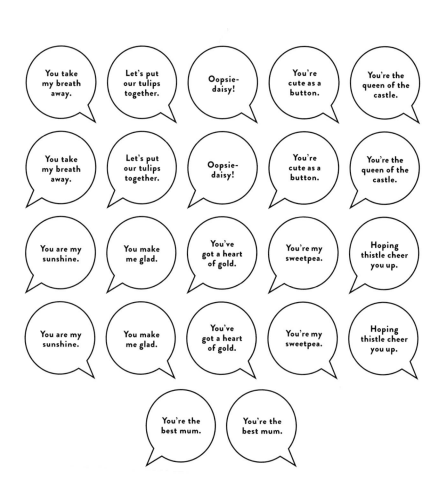

Fill-in-the-Blank Tattoos

PAGE 39, ENLARGE 200%

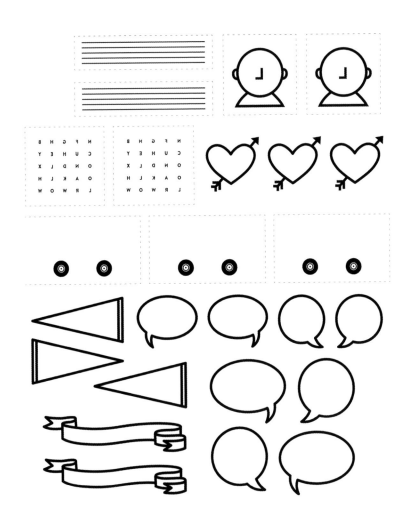

Everyday Advent

PAGE 43, ENLARGE 200%

You're my favorite little monster.

YOU TURN MY FROWN ↓ UPSIDE DOWN

I think you're dino-mite!

"EYE" LOVE YOU

You're so fly.

HAVE A SWEET DAY

Yay! You rule!

This coupon is good for:

Breakfast in bed

This coupon is good for:

A back rub

This coupon is good for:

1 hour of quiet time

This coupon is good for:

A coffee break

This coupon is good for:

1 car wash

This coupon is good for:

A movie date

This coupon is good for:

2 loads of laundry

Personal Storybook (Template 1 of 4)

All About

_____
(your name)

(Front Cover)

By

_____
(your name)

(Back Cover)

Hi!
My name is _____.
I am _____.
My eyes are _____,
and my hair is _____.

(Page 1)

Draw
your face
here!

(Page 2)

(Page 3)

In the summer, I like
_____.
In the spring, I enjoy
_____.
In the fall, I go _____
_____.
In the winter, I love
_____.

↖
*What do you
love most about
each season?*

(Page 4)

My family is _____
_____.
We like to _____
together.
My friends are _____
_____.
We like to _____
together.

↗
*Draw
your favorite
people in
these frames!*

(Page 5)

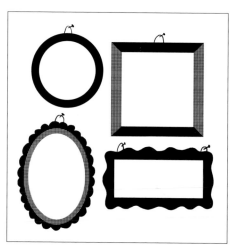

(Page 6)

Draw your favorite meal!

(Page 7)

I love to eat
_____
and _____.
I would eat
_____
everyday if I
could!

(Page 8)

I live in _____.
In my neighborhood I
see _____ and
_____.

(Page 9)

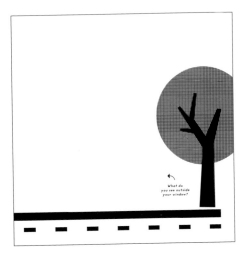

What do you see outside your window?

(Page 10)

171

What do you
wish for?

(Page 11)

When I grow up, I want
to _____.
My dream is to _____
_____.

(Page 12)

Coffee Sampler

PAGE 55, ENLARGE 200%

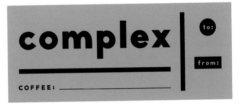

173

174

happy

Brighten up your mood with
cheerful **LEMON TEA.**

bashful

Tame your timid nerves with
calming **LAVENDER TEA.**

sleepy

Perk up with a perfect cup
of **ENGLISH BREAKFAST TEA.**

grumpy

Turn that frown
upside down with soothing
CHAMOMILE TEA.

Tea Sampler *(Template 2 of 2)*

PAGE 59, ENLARGE 200%

sneezy

Gesundheit!
Get rid of sniffles and sneezes
with restorative GINGER TEA.

dopey

Boost your sluggish memory and
brain health with energizing
GREEN TEA.

doc

Remedy tummy troubles
with PEPPERMINT TEA — it's just
what the doctor ordered.

Candy Board Games: CHINESE CHECKERS

PAGE 67, ENLARGE 350% AND TILE

Candy Board Games: CAT AND MOUSE CHASE

PAGE 69, ENLARGE 350% AND TILE

Candy Board Games: TIC-TAC-TOE

PAGE 69, ENLARGE 200%

Bike Dates *(Template 1 of 2)*

PAGE 75, ENLARGE 250%

Bike Dates *(Template 2 of 2)*

DESTINATION:

STARTING POINT

↓

TOTAL TRAVEL TIME

↓

1. _____   11. _____
2. _____   12. _____
3. _____   13. _____
4. _____   14. _____
5. _____   15. _____
6. _____   16. _____
7. _____   17. _____
8. _____   18. _____
9. _____   19. _____
10. _____   20. _____

STARTING POINT: ➤   DESTINATION:

Macaron Messages

PAGE 83, ENLARGE 250%

BOX SLIDING COVER

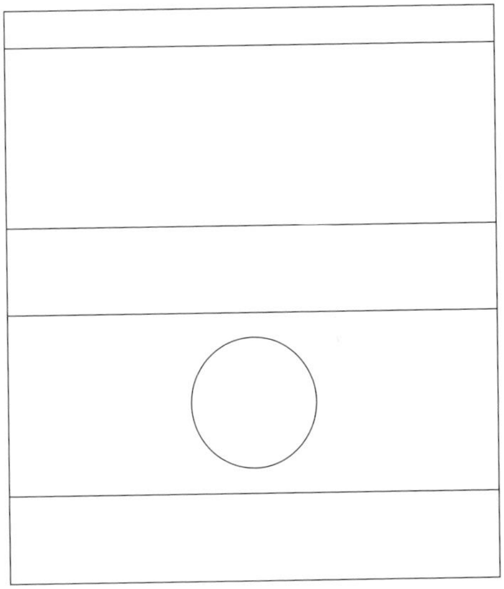

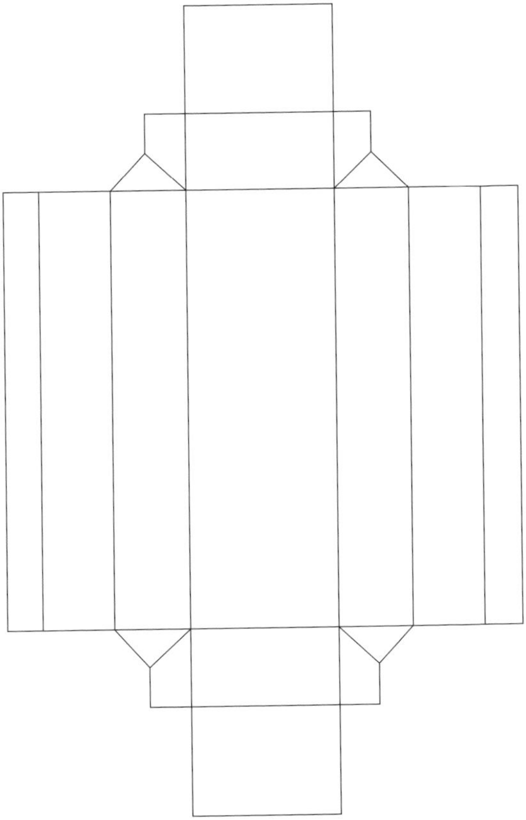

181

BOX BOTTOM

Custom Growler

PAGE 87, ENLARGE 185%

Trompe L'oeil Shoes

PAGE 95, ENLARGE 250%

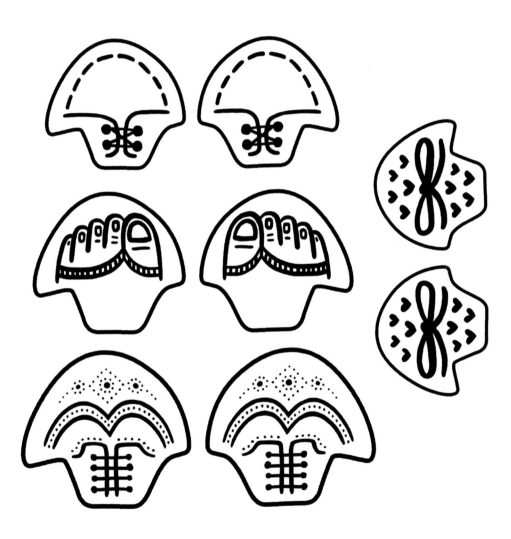

Lavender Cloud Sachets

PAGE 99, ENLARGE 200%

Rebus Wall Hanging

PAGE 111, ENLARGE 250%

Scratch-Off Calendar *(Template 1 of 4)*

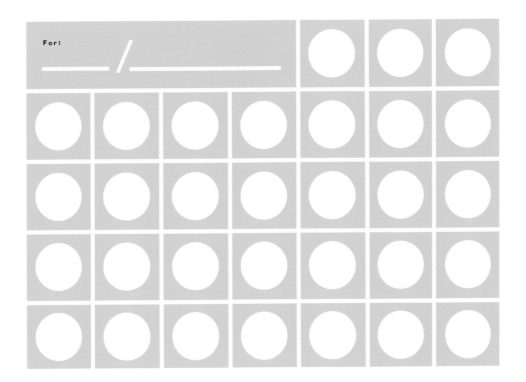

For: _____ / _____

Scratch-Off Calendar *(Template 2 of 4)*

PAGE 115, ENLARGE 200%

For: ____ / ________				1	Gray's Papaya	Bemelman's cocktails
4	Staten Island ferry	6	Katz's pastrami	picnic in Central Park	9	walk the High Line
Chinatown dim sum	12	donut crawl	jazz at Village Vanguard	15	photo booth at Ace Hotel	17
18	walk across the Brooklyn Bridge	20	trip to the Guggenheim	bagels and lox at Russ & Sons	23	Brooklyn Flea
slice of pizza at Joe's	outdoor movie at Bryant Park	27	dinner at Freemans	29	Comedy Cellar set	31

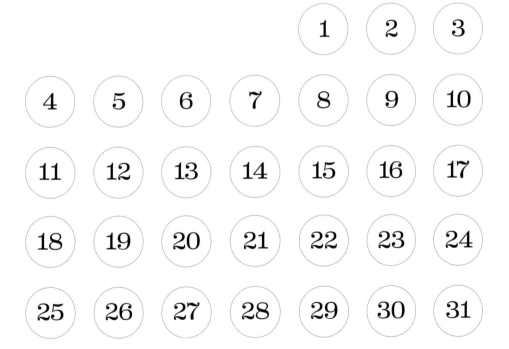

go to _____	farmers' market	cocktails	let's _____	road trip	Gray's Papaya	MoMA	Katz's pastrami	Union Sq Greenmarket
art gallery	flea market	beers	bike ride	ferry ride	Bemelman's cocktails	outdoor movie at Bryant Park	Staten Island Ferry	bagels and lox at Russ & Sons
museum trip	theatre show	burgers	picnic	dim sum	dinner at Freemans	photo booth at Ace Hotel	Brooklyn Flea	slice of pizza at Joe's
ball game	go to the beach	donuts	dance party	coffee date	Chinatown dim sum	ice skating at Rockefeller Center	walk across the Brooklyn Bridge	Comedy Cellar set
movie date	music concert	pizza	ice skating	hiking	walk the High Line	donut crawl	Jane's Carousel	jazz at Village Vanguard
visit the park	eat _____	ice cream	bake cookies	camping	Empire State Building	picnic in Central Park	burger at Shake Shack	gelato in the West Village

188

189

191

Yearbook Photo Album

PAGE 127, ENLARGE 100%

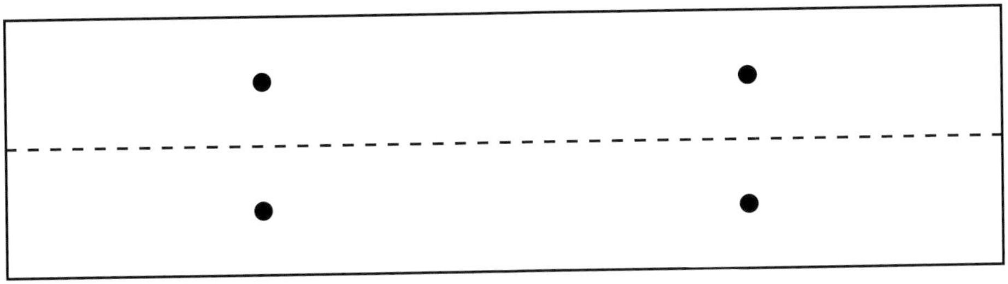

BINDING TEMPLATE

Thank-You Wallet *(Template 1 of 2)*

PAGE 131, ENLARGE 165%

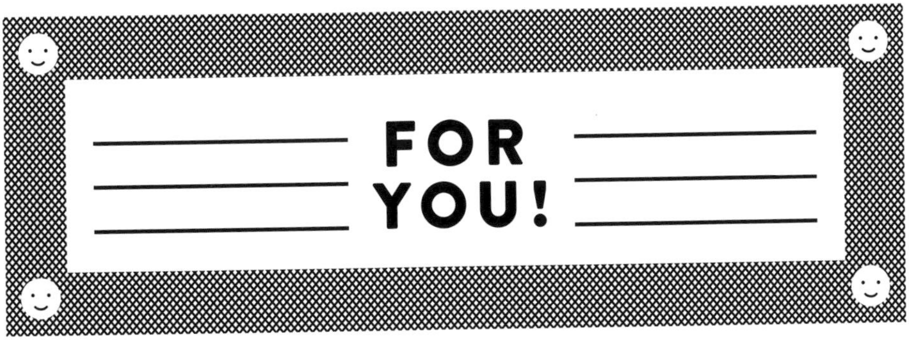

FOR
YOU!

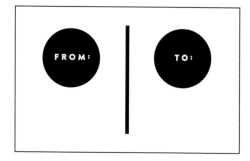

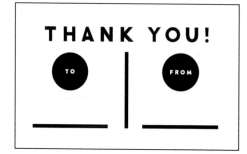

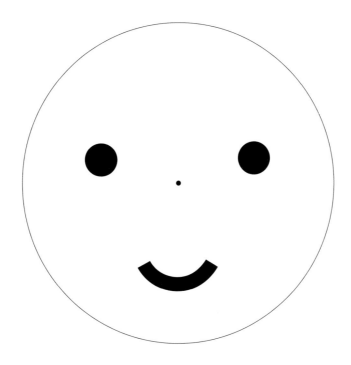

195

Perpetual Greeting (Template 1 of 5)

PAGE 151, ENLARGE 165%

I

you

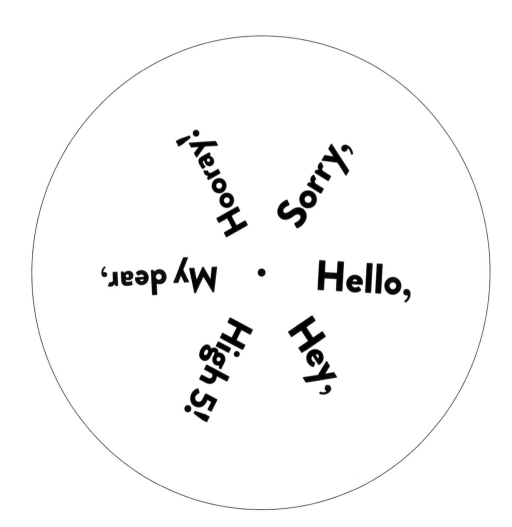

198

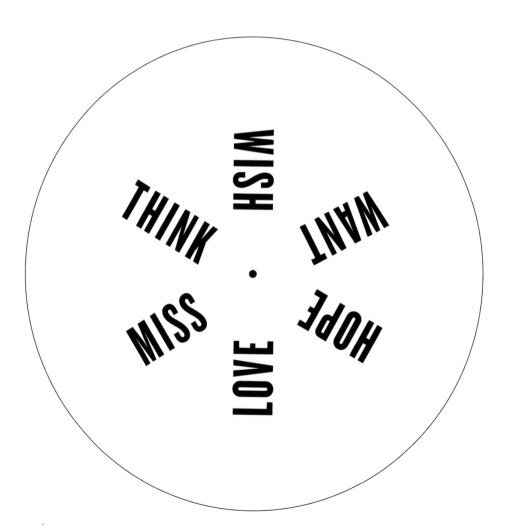

Perpetual Greeting (Template 4 of 5)

PAGE 151, ENLARGE 165%

199

are the
bee's knees

like crazy

more than the
moon & stars

forgive me

all the best

the most

Perpetual Greeting *(Template 5 of 5)*

PAGE 151, ENLARGE 400% AND TILE

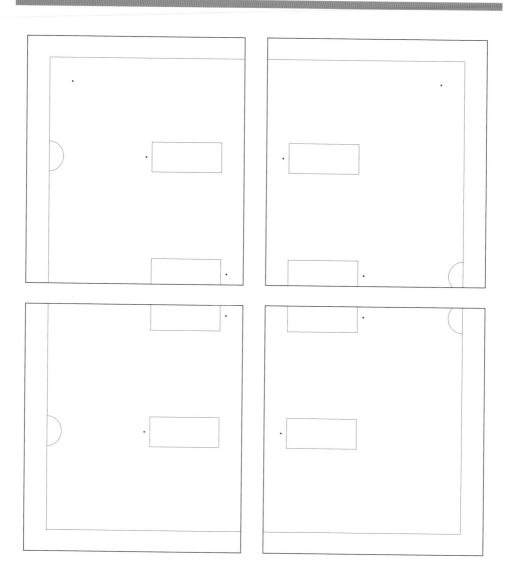

200

The Ultimate Desk Surprise

PAGE 154, SCAN AND SAVE TO DESKTOP DIMENSIONS

SMALL
GABLE BOX
(FRONT)

SMALL
GABLE BOX
(SIDES)

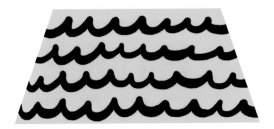

MEDIUM GABLE BOX
(FRONT)

MEDIUM GABLE BOX
(SIDES)

LARGE GABLE BOX
(FRONT)

LARGE GABLE BOX
(SIDES)

Thank You

We are completely indebted to the people who helped us along the way. You are the mac to our cheese, the milk to our cookies, the bread to our butter. Thank you so much!

WON
My sister, whose support and advice was invaluable to the book

ABE
"You're the top, you're my devotion, bossa nova dream..."

SARA
Our editor, and most serendipitous dinner companion

JUDY
Our agent-extraordinaire

MABEL & FRED
My parents and #1 fans

MILES
My sunshine, may you grow to love making and giving

SUN & HWEE
My parents, my biggest cheerleaders

OLIVER
My big brother and childhood conspirator

J & NATE, DYLAN & OMI
The coolest kids I know, always inspiring new projects

KIT & RICHARD
My cousins whose hospitality is second to none

MARCIE
My mentor and lucky break

GINA & C.C.
Loving babysitters

BLAKE
Our dear friend and generous craft-tool-lender

MEI & JANG
My in-laws and examples in generosity

NINA
Our wordsmith and naming expert

And all our creative friends and family who continually inspire and support us!